I Am Enough

by

Jennifer D. Calvin

authorHOUSE

1663 LIBERTY DRIVE, SUITE 200
BLOOMINGTON, INDIANA 47403
(800) 839-8640
WWW.AUTHORHOUSE.COM

This book is a work of non-fiction. Unless otherwise noted, the author and the publisher make no explicit guarantees as to the accuracy of the information contained in this book and in some cases, names of people and places have been altered to protect their privacy.

© 2005 Jennifer D. Calvin. All Rights Reserved.

No part of this book may be reproduced, stored in a retrieval system, or transmitted by any means without the written permission of the author.

First published by AuthorHouse 04/04/05

ISBN: 1-4208-3708-7 (e)
ISBN: 1-4208-3707-9 (sc)

Printed in the United States of America
Bloomington, Indiana

This book is printed on acid-free paper.

To Matt, Mom, Dad, and Karyn—
Thank you for believing in me.

Chapter One

"The Road"

My road is a long one with no clear end in sight.
It's generally a gradual up-slope with occasional steep hills.
As I travel, I meet forks in the road that are unclearly marked.
I am easily confused as I am faced with making a decision as to which direction to proceed.
The path is clear only occasionally.
I meet constant obstacles.
At times there is loose gravel on which I slip.
Other times, boulders stand in my way.
I tread over muddy ground.
I hide in the fog at times and fight through stormy weather.
There are hills and valleys and rough terrain.
Ditches and danger zones go unmarked, and I often find myself in them without warning.
This road is a difficult one to travel.
Will it ever be smooth, flat, and clearly marked?
Do I, or should I, want it to be that way?
My only hope is that God will lead me.
He knows my road well, even when it seems I'm traveling it alone.

11/19/03

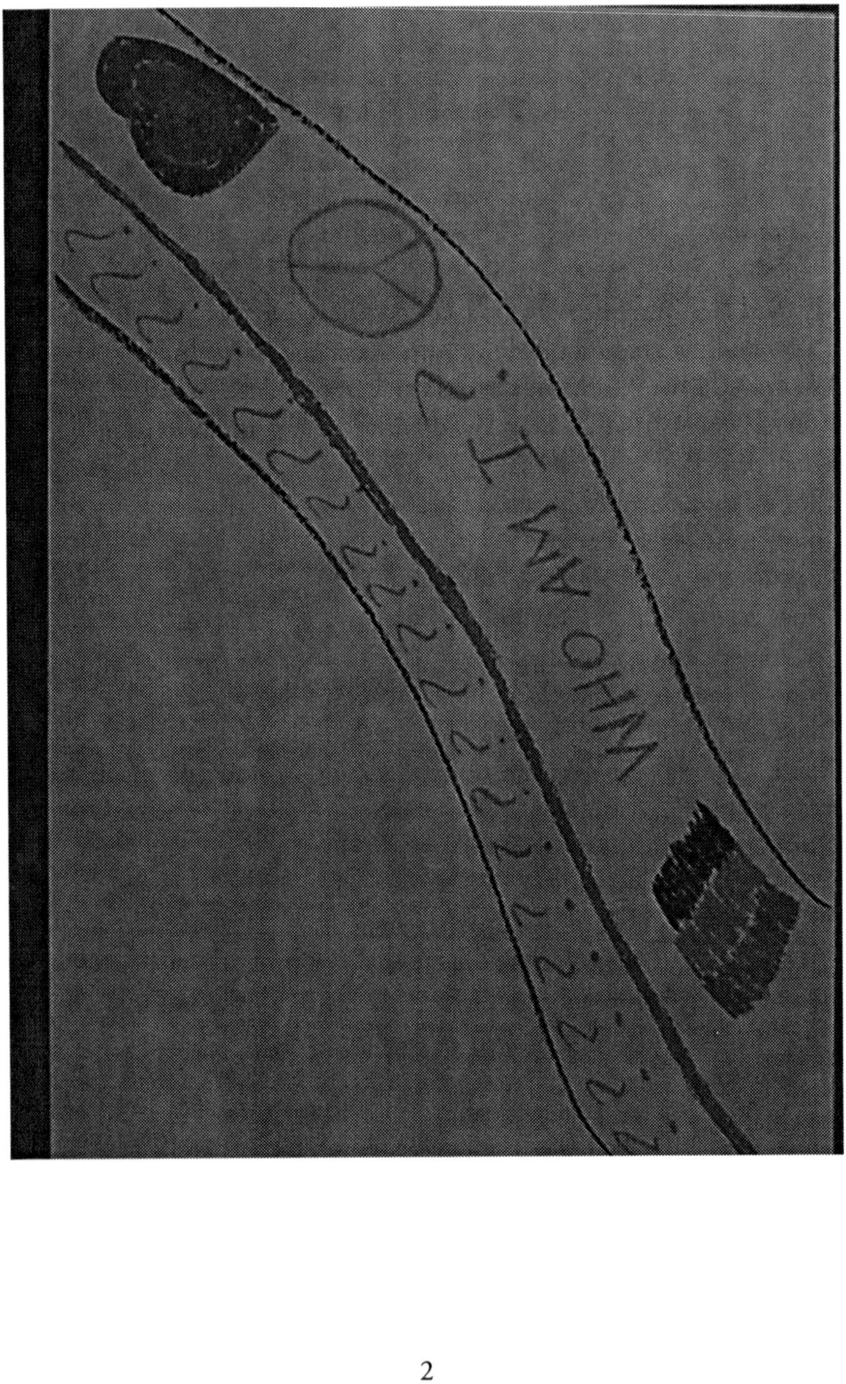
WHO AM I?

My eating disorder did not surface when I was a young teenager. It did not result from one traumatic experience in my life. As I know it now, the onset was gradual, resulting from numerous factors throughout my life. The first eating disordered thought I remember occurred in 1993 before I left for my freshman year of college at Saint Louis University. The thought went something like this, "O God, please do not let me come back home from college for the first time having gained the 'freshman fifteen'."

I was absolutely terrified of what people would think of me if I returned home from college for the first time being any heavier than I was before I left. And I was not heavy. I weighed a normal body weight for my height and had never worried before about such things—at least consciously.

I grew up in what I thought was the perfect family, with the perfect parents, the perfect sister, and the most perfect childhood a kid could ever have. I don't think I had ever truly realized that any of the four of us were human. The Lanes? Human?? Surely not! That would mean that we were flawed. On an individual level, that would mean that I had limitations. Growing up as I had, believing that I could do anything I wanted to do and be anything I wanted to be, the thought of my having limitations was foreign.

Even though I grew up in a household with a mom who dealt with an undiagnosed eating disorder but didn't believe that her issues affected our family and a dad who ignored her cries for help because he simply didn't know how to deal with them, I thought our family was just about as perfect as one could be. I, as the oldest child, had no idea about the messages that I received subconsciously as I grew up.

My life as a child felt very happy. My mom stayed home full-time with my younger sister, Karyn, and me. We were always on the go, as my parents felt it very important that Karyn and I be exposed to numerous activities. We went skating at the roller rink, visited the library quite frequently, attended plays at the children's theater, and were extremely involved in church activities.

Mom was always available, and that felt so good. I felt so loved and knew that she would always be there (at least physically) whenever I needed her. She was a room mother, school volunteer, PTA member, church organist, etc., etc., etc. She wore so many hats that I am amazed now at how she "kept it all together." As a child, I thought this was "normal" for a mom. I now realize that she had her own ways of dealing with stress, and they weren't as perfect as I thought she was.

My mom lived with a secret that no one outside our immediate family knew about. At least we didn't think anyone else had caught on. She lived within the obsessive world of an eating disorder. It began for her when her obstetrician told her she shouldn't gain too much weight during pregnancy. And she was not overweight to begin with. That comment led my mom into a spiral of restriction that, thirty years later, she is just beginning to reverse.

From my perspective as a child, her world seemed ruled by the scale. And my perspective was accurate. Her day was made or broken by what the scale showed every morning. And it continued to be made or broken throughout the day by what the scale read at different times. I remember watching her agonize over the numbers—a feeling I know all too well now. She was trapped. She defined herself and her self worth by whatever number on which the needle landed.

Without consciously realizing it, I believe I felt such sadness for her. She was "my perfect mom." She didn't deserve to be so unhappy. She shouldn't have to hate herself and her body. She was wonderful—and still is. Everyone else believed it. Why didn't she? I wanted to save her from her self-torture. I wanted to make her happy. I wanted to take her pain away. The question became, "how would I accomplish that?" The answer was, "by being the perfect child."

I didn't even realize what was occurring in my brain. I didn't consciously think to myself, "I need to step up and do things perfectly so Mom will feel proud of me and be happy with herself that she raised such a good kid." But subconsciously, these are the exact thoughts that permeated my young mind. None of us knew what was subconsciously occurring.

***

I remember separating from my mom felt somewhat traumatic. I hated leaving her when she would drop me off at pre-school. I cried, and cried, and cried. On some level, I must have feared abandonment. Kindergarten did not seem to give me as many problems as did pre-school, but when first grade rolled around, my separation issues flared up again. Mom was called to school numerous times because I would not stop crying until she came. I remember my lunch meat sandwiches being ruined from tears. I wanted to be with her so badly. Just as I subconsciously wanted to relieve her pain, she very consciously desired to alleviate mine.

My parents have maintained a very strong marriage for thirty-five years. It has not gone without its rocky times, but it has always remained rooted in Christ Jesus. I am thankful beyond measure for the Christian upbringing my parents provided for me. Even though God has always been on their side, their relationship has faced its challenges.

My dad worked all day in the world of finance while Mom cared all day for Karyn and me. Roles seemed very defined. Dad worked to make the money to pay the bills while Mom worked to keep the house in complete order. Dad mowed the lawn while Mom weeded and clipped. Dad fixed things while Mom told him what needed to be fixed. It felt very "Leave It To Beaverish" to me. It was comfortable and just the way I wanted it to always be. "Normalcy" in our family also included Mom's restrictive eating patterns.

I always knew my parents loved each other, despite the fact that I very rarely saw them show affection for each other. A goodbye or hello peck seemed normal, but anything beyond that I deemed as "gross." The "gross" times were few and far between. I almost couldn't bear to watch the rare occasions that they would hold hands. And I remember that, fortunately or unfortunately, I never had the experience of "walking in on my parents." I think I would have been mortified had that ever happened to me.

Dad was the quiet, reserved, shy one of the two of them, while Mom appeared to be the more outgoing, talkative one. Mom needed Dad to hear her and talk with her. He just didn't know how. I believe she really did try, at times, to use her voice with Dad. But he didn't hear her. Thus, she began to starve herself to make him hear. He still didn't.

I remember lying in bed in the mornings hearing Mom and Dad talking in the garage before Dad left for work. Through the vents, I all-too-often heard Mom crying, trying to express her emotions and feelings. It seemed like Dad never knew what to say to help her feel better. In all actuality, that wasn't his job anyway. She needed to know how to help herself feel better.

I could hear Mom's footsteps up the stairs after Dad left. I so desperately wanted to take away her pain. Her puffy, red eyes made my heart hurt for her. All I knew to do in these moments was to get ready for school quietly and in the least obtrusive way I knew how. I hoped this would please Mom and help her to feel better.

* * *

My parents are among the most supportive I've ever seen. They would do anything for Karyn and me. It seems as though they love us more than they love themselves. Throughout my life, they have always been around, and I have loved this. Many kids would have felt embarrassed that they attended virtually every school activity I was ever involved in. But I felt so blessed that my parents cared enough to come and support me when many of my friends' parents were never around.

While the attention from my mom and dad was so wonderful, I also developed serious separation issues with them. My parents became my conscience. I made decisions based on what I thought they would do or what they would think was the best way to go. I was afraid to decide for myself. I was terrified to think for myself about what I might want. I think I feared rejection or disapproval from my parents if my decisions didn't jive with what they would have done. Thus, I was developing a serious identity crisis, and I didn't even know it was occurring.

I never tested my parents with my behavior. I feared letting them down, and I feared feeling their disapproval. Anger was very rarely projected onto me. I grew up to be a severe people-pleaser. I did what I thought everyone else wanted me to do. I did what I thought I should do. What is it that I want to do? This question rarely entered my mind.

Of course, I participated in activities that I enjoyed, but I wanted to succeed to make Mom and Dad pleased more than for my own satisfaction. I knew that if I did well and achieved great things, they would feel proud of not only me but of themselves because they had raised such a great and successful child. My parents never expressed their personal need for me to do well. However, numerous academic awards, musical achievements, and athletic successes of mine helped us each feel "good" for our own reasons. Little did we realize how intertwined they all were.

Mom and Dad's incredible and best intentions in helping me be involved in so many different activities was to help me, in turn, develop a personal identity. What actually occurred was a false sense of identity, based on what I did and not who I was. I was so busy doing that I never learned what it meant to truly just "be." I am now, at age twenty-nine, trying to find my "being identity." No blame is placed on anyone. Mom and Dad did what they thought was best. Their intentions were the most loving they could have ever been.

My parents' love is amazing. They sacrificed their own personal relationship, their social relationships and so much more so that my sister and I knew beyond a reasonable doubt that we were loved. I love my parents dearly for this. But I hold a sadness in my heart for them that they sacrificed themselves. Their own fulfillment is so incredibly important.

Chapter Two

"My body"

My body—
I see it as ugly and gross.
My body—
I definitely don't want to boast.

My body—
It feels so disgustingly fat.
My body—
My stomach just isn't flat.

My body—
I can't tell if I'm hungry or full.
My body—
Might feel better if it was run over by a bull.

My body—
It shivers and shakes in the cold.
My body—
Blankets and sweaters are welcomed as gold.

My body—
It's numb to the touch of a man.
My body—
It hates to feel food in my hand.

My body—
The nastiness rages within.
My body—
Is what I'm doing to it completely a sin?

9/13/03

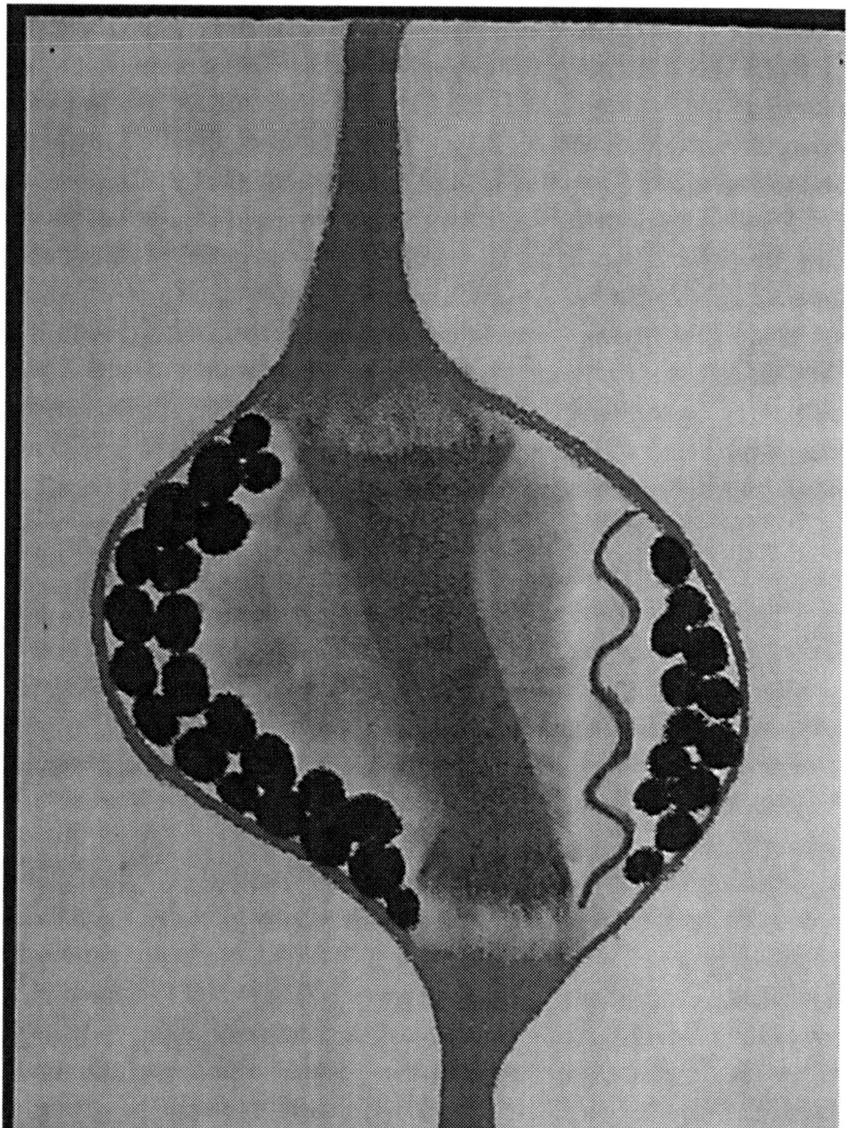

In junior high, my obsessive thinking really began to reveal itself. As a younger child, I had an intense fear of vomiting. In seventh grade, this fear began to transfer itself into fear and obsessive thoughts of suicide. I remember being scared to walk into the kitchen fearing that I would lose control and kill myself with the knives. The same type of fear plagued me each time I passed the hall closet containing my mom's sewing scissors. I had such fear within me that I would lie in my bed and shake. I remember Karyn sitting with me, holding my hand and telling me that I would be okay. To this day, she reassures me.

My obsessive worries and thoughts landed me in counseling for the first time when I was in the seventh grade. I hated going—absolutely dreaded it. My parents had to bribe me to go by taking me to lunch at *Pizza Hut* each time. I remember sitting as far away as I could from the doctor—way down at the far end of the infamous couch. I was terrified of having to verbalize my fears to a stranger. The work I did was positive and did help me to learn how to quiet the voices in my head, causing the thoughts to subside.

***

High school was a very happy and enjoyable time for me. I had several groups of friends, both younger and older than myself. I was extremely active in sports, music, and academics. There always seemed to be some kind of award or achievement for which to strive. This was a point in my life when I very strongly, but very subconsciously, wanted to please my parents, my teachers, and myself. I played the part of "the good girl" very well.

Although I was constantly participating in activities, I didn't have much of a social life outside of school functions. I didn't care about going to the popular parties or having a date each weekend or a steady boyfriend. I was perfectly happy to spend a Friday night at home with my family. I wish I had challenged myself more socially at that stage of my life. I also wish I had tested my parents' temper a little more. Instead, I'm trying to rebel in many ways now as an adult.

I don't remember worrying about what I ate or how my body looked in high school. I think I was fairly confident and happy in my own skin. The people with whom I surrounded myself were very healthy both in their eating habits and lifestyles, so I had good models. I do remember examining myself in the mirror several different times and focusing on my stomach/waist area. However, it didn't seem to me to be anything abnormal for a girl my age.

I became very interested in exploring the world of physical therapy during my high school years, so I volunteered at clinics during summers. My senior year of high school, I was accepted into the physical therapy program at Saint Louis University. In August, 1993, I was off to St. Louis, Missouri.

Chapter Three

"Ambivalence"

Which road do I take?
Which way do I turn?
I cannot decide
Which way my heart yearns.

I need a clear path.
My vision is blurred.
I cannot yet tell
Which way my heart stirs.

One arrow points north.
One arrow points south.
My mind feels so hazy
And blurred with the clouds.

What will it take
For me to decide?
I cannot just stop
And curl up and hide.

9/14/03

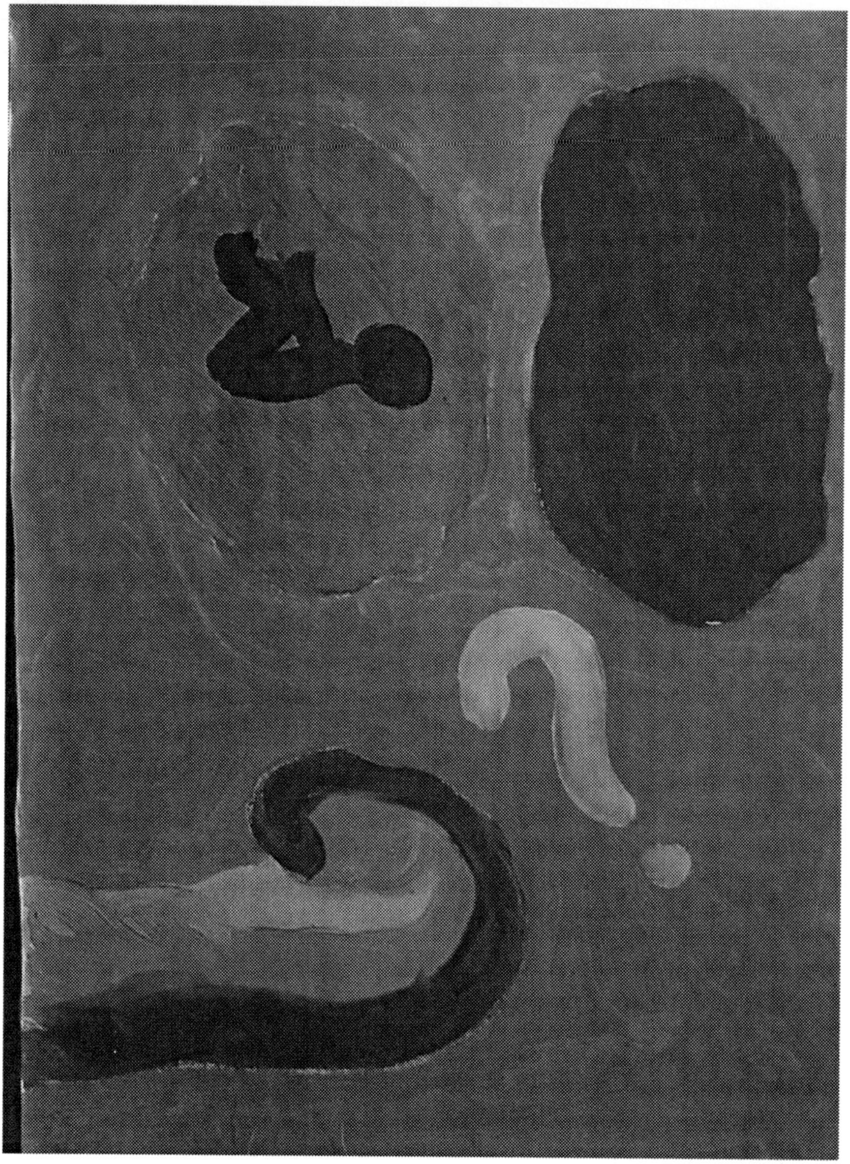

Jennifer D. Calvin

The week my parents and sister moved me to SLU was filled with emotion. I felt like I was in tears most of the time and just didn't want to leave the safe haven of my parents' protection. I knew I was scared. And this is one reason that I knew I needed to go away from home for college. I needed to begin to develop my own identity. I really thought I would be able to do this. Thinking back now at age twenty-nine to this point in my life, I think I may have been just as afraid for my parents being left without me to focus on now as much as I was afraid of being without them. Would they be okay?

I would not describe college as being "the best years of my life." I have no desire to re-live those five and a half years. It was during these years that my eating disorder tendencies began to truly show themselves. I became self-conscious about foods I chose to eat when I sat down one day at the table, and the girl across from me said, "I can't believe you're going to drink that 2% milk! The skim is so much healthier for you." These types of comments, coupled with my fear of returning home for the first time having gained the "freshman fifteen" made me begin to gravitate toward more "health foods." In reality, they are diet foods, and I had no reason at the time to require myself to choose them over non-diet foods. Peer pressure, societal expectations, and my own drive to be "as healthy as possible" began to affect me. I began to increase my running regimen as I feared not having the two-hour after-school athletic practice anymore. Little did I realize that my own personal workouts were filled with more activity than were my high-school practices.

I viewed my new-found eating patterns as "I'm being more healthy." I remember my mom being very surprised when I asked her to have skim milk on hand now when I would come home. I was restricting when I had no reason to, and I didn't realize it. I did return home for the first time in October, 1993, not having gained the "freshman fifteen," and feeling very proud of that. In fact, I was probably a little thinner than I was when I left for college.

I was very driven in my college years to succeed academically as best I could. I was working my way through a very demanding science-based curriculum that set high expectations for all of us as students. The margin for error was small. Added to that, I was one of approximately eighty over-achieving, competitive, perfectionistic students. We each pushed the other to incredible limits. Needless to say, I was extremely stressed out for approximately five years.

Looking back on my college years, they seemed to consist of studying, studying, and more studying as well as working out, with socializing being one of the areas I focused on the least. I told myself, "I'm not here to have fun. I am here to study and get the highest grades I can." I want to make it clear that this is what I told *myself*. It is not what my *parents* told me. In fact, my dad said to me numerous times, "Jen, I'll pay you if you will just get a C." They understood the amount of pressure I put on myself.

I developed a couple of friendships that remain very close to my heart and special to this day. I am incredibly thankful for them. During college, I did not feel particularly strong in my social skills and feared, subconsciously, letting anyone get too close to me. I didn't want friendships to interfere with my study habits.

* * *

Toward the end of my sophomore year, I became very good friends with another girl at SLU. We had a great deal in common with each other. Little did I know that as we started becoming friends, she was in the midst of developing an eating disorder. We developed what I am now able to see was a very dependent relationship. We would care-take for each other. We each felt good that we needed each other. I didn't see my friend's behaviors as being destructive in the beginning, but as time went on, it became very clear to me that she had serious problems that needed attention. She was the first outside exposure I'd had to the world of eating disorders, aside from growing up in a household with an eating disordered person.

There came a time when my friend was worrying about ingesting water. It was at this point that I knew something had to be done. I remember telling her that I wanted her to go see the university psychologist. She fought the idea, but I knew the circumstances were beyond what I knew how to handle as a friend. I was exhausted. I felt I needed to go to her room numerous times during the day just to make sure she was alive. It felt good that she needed and depended upon me. I couldn't take care of her on my own anymore. Finally, she agreed to go talk to the psychologist, but only if I would go with her.

So, we went together. I remember experiencing such relief that I didn't need to feel responsible for her anymore. At least someone else knew what was going on.

This situation completely drained our friendship. We slowly grew further and further apart. I know she got worse before getting better, but I do not know where or how she is today. I learned a great deal from this relationship, but unfortunately, it was one that needed to end. This terrible disease has a way of ruining not only our health but our relationships as well.

Interestingly enough, I seem to have been drawn to people with disordered eating. During my college years, I encountered and oftentimes became friends with several people with disordered eating habits. I had a great need to care-take. Meeting other people's needs and making others happy made me feel good about myself. I felt useful, needed, and worthy by care-taking. What I didn't realize was that it was a false sense of worthiness. I didn't know how to make *myself* feel useful, needed, and worthy. I didn't believe I was worthy just because I was me.

* * *

During my senior year, I became depressed to the point that I needed to enter counseling. I was able to recognize the symptoms in myself and asked my parents for help. I felt so trapped by school, studying, and my perfectionistic nature. Food had nothing to do with my depression at this point. I was isolating myself to study and didn't know how to get myself out of the quicksand that I was sinking further into.

My parents found me a therapist at home in Kansas City. I would fly home every other Friday to attend a session with my therapist and then would stay home the rest of the weekend. The time away from my school environment did wonders for me. It was good for me to be able to more regularly physically connect with my family as well.

The therapy did wonders for me at that point. I learned to do quite a bit with self-talk and turning negative thoughts into positive ones. I learned to relax and lighten up on myself a bit. I developed a healthier attitude toward the experience of college that I wish I had developed much earlier than my senior year. After a few months of counseling,

I was enjoying my life much more. I felt like I had done good work during my therapy. I came to realize that grades were not the end-all-be-all of my existence and that the experience of life would offer me much more in the end than would the honors with which I graduated. I lightened up on the amount and intensity of my studying and did just as well academically.

I think the most important thing I gained from that therapy was a more positive self-esteem. I began to like myself more and feel more confident as an individual. I started participating more socially and saw that I was capable of enjoying myself. I was much more at ease socially. I wasn't as afraid of letting people get to know me.

At one point I was very depressed that I was not seriously dating a guy. Friends of mine were starting to get engaged, and I was SURE that I would NEVER get married. Who could love me enough that he would want to spend his entire life with my miserable self? Through the work I did in counseling with becoming more confident with myself, I reached a point where I was very comfortable with the idea that I could be happy and live a fulfilled life even if I never did get married. This was a very critical point for me to reach. Ironically, once I wholeheartedly believed this about myself, I suddenly became much more open and comfortable with guys. I realized that I could have close relationships with guys even if they didn't lead to marriage. Dating was suddenly much easier and more fun.

* * *

At the end of my senior year, I attended a retreat called SLU Encounter. This turned out to be a very pivotal point in my individual spiritual life. I had felt for a while that I was in a drought spiritually. I remember discussing with a friend of mine how neither one of us was too excited about going. We were both complaining about the amount of studying we needed to do that weekend and how we just didn't feel like we had the time to devote to this retreat. We both ended up going, putting our studying aside, and giving ourselves the time with God. We have since agreed that it was one of the best decisions of our lives. It was one of the first times that I remember truly sitting with God and spending concentrated time with Him. He touched me in a very special way that weekend, as did other Christians on the retreat and those who had written me notes of encouragement. During one of the prayer services, I truly repented my sins like I had never done before. I felt God touch me and cleanse me. I yearn, again, to feel His presence in me like that.

Tammy Trent's song "Welcome Home" spoke to me so loudly at this time in my life. I felt like I had strayed from God. She sings ". . . there's no shame in your returning though you may have wandered far. Welcome home." Those words reminded me that God loves me unconditionally no matter where I am in my life. He will always welcome me home into His arms.

Chapter Four

"Time"

My monster grew up slowly over time.
I didn't even know it was a part of me for quite some time.
We gradually became acquainted.
It told me I should run more and convert to "lite" and "reduced fat" this and that.
Its pictures began to take up permanent residence in my mind.

We gradually began spending more and more time together.
We ran more and ate less.
It felt good.
I came to want to spend even more time with my monster.
It became my friend—or so I thought.
A means of control and security.

Before long, my monster began demanding too much of my time.
It began controlling me instead of my controlling it.
It took away my time—from myself, my relationships, and my life.
It's time for me to start reclaiming my time.
I deserve time.
Time to heal, recover, grow, explore.
Time for me.

10/10/03

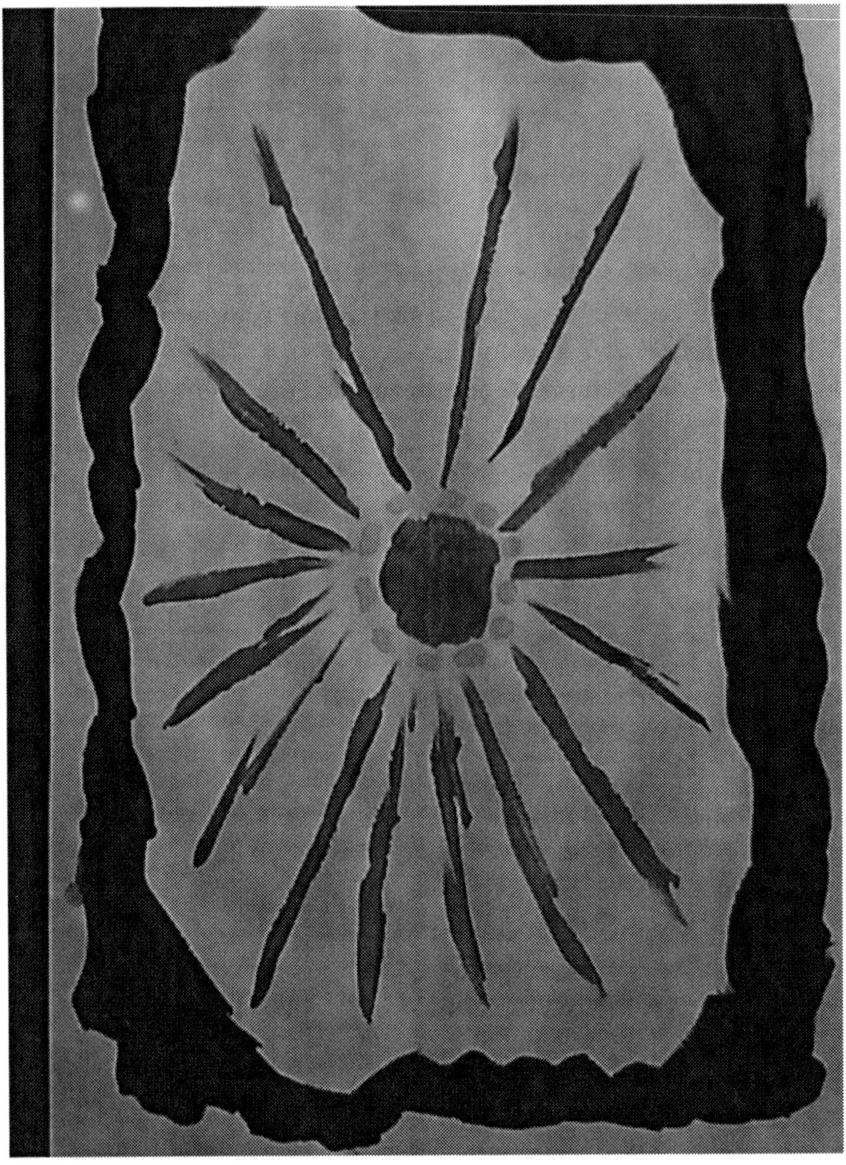

I finished the class work portion of my curriculum in July, 1998. I had a semester of clinicals to complete and would graduate with my Master's in Physical Therapy in December, 1998. My first clinical was at the University of Nebraska-Lincoln, where my sister was an undergraduate. While on this six-week clinical, I began dating my now-husband, Matt.

Our story is very special in that we grew up going to the same church in Kansas City, Missouri. We developed a friendship that lasted throughout high school and college. We would see each other socially on breaks, but nothing romantic had ever happened, much to my dismay. I had had quite a crush on Matt since junior high, but I had never been able to attract his attention in that way. I was always too embarrassed and insecure to reveal my feelings to him.

Surprisingly, one night before I left Kansas City to travel to Lincoln to begin my clinical, Matt asked me what had been going on between us for all these years. I was absolutely shocked that he had any romantic feelings for me! At the time, he was getting ready to return to Concordia University in Seward, Nebraska, only about twenty minutes from Lincoln. The timing couldn't have been more perfect. I would be in Lincoln for six weeks, and this would give us a chance to see each other more frequently.

The first actual date that we consider ourselves having gone on was so special. We spent most of the night engaged in conversation like we'd never had before. I opened up to him about my struggles, insecurities, and counseling sessions. It was a freeing experience for me to be honest with him about my true self. He admitted that he was amazed at what I had told him as he'd always seen me as being popular, confident, secure, having everything together. Our relationship moved to a different level that night because of the honesty and acceptance that had been created between us. The night ended with our praying together, asking God to take our relationship in His hands and lead us according to His will as we were both uncertain of what the future held.

* * *

I traveled on to Shreveport, Louisiana, for my second clinical. At this time, I was cautious about what I ate, but I was very healthy. Exercise was continually becoming more of a "have to."

I finished my clinicals in Chicago. Matt came to visit me the first weekend of this last clinical, and after that weekend, it was safe to say that we were an item. While in Chicago, I fell in love with the city. I decided it was one place in which I definitely wanted to look for a job after graduation.

I knew I didn't want to settle in Kansas City after graduation. I needed to strike out on my own in a new city with new surroundings as I feared staying in Kansas City and risking crawling right back into my parents' safe cocoon. That would only be playing with fire. I needed to show myself that I could stand on my own two feet and be okay in my own world, even though I was scared to death.

I job searched for four months at home before finding a job in Chicago. I moved in April, 1999, into my own apartment in the western suburbs. I felt confident, strong, and excited along with feeling insecure, nervous, and anxious. It was good to be on my own.

Chapter Five

"Will I Eat?"

Will I choose to eat
When I'm on my own?
I just don't know.
I really don't know!

I want to restrict.
My urges are there.
I want to feel empty.
Do I dare? Do I dare?

I feel I should run.
I feel I should sweat
To shed these few pounds
And put my body back in debt.

I don't want to eat
To take care of myself.
What will I do?
I'm teetering on a shelf.

9/15/03

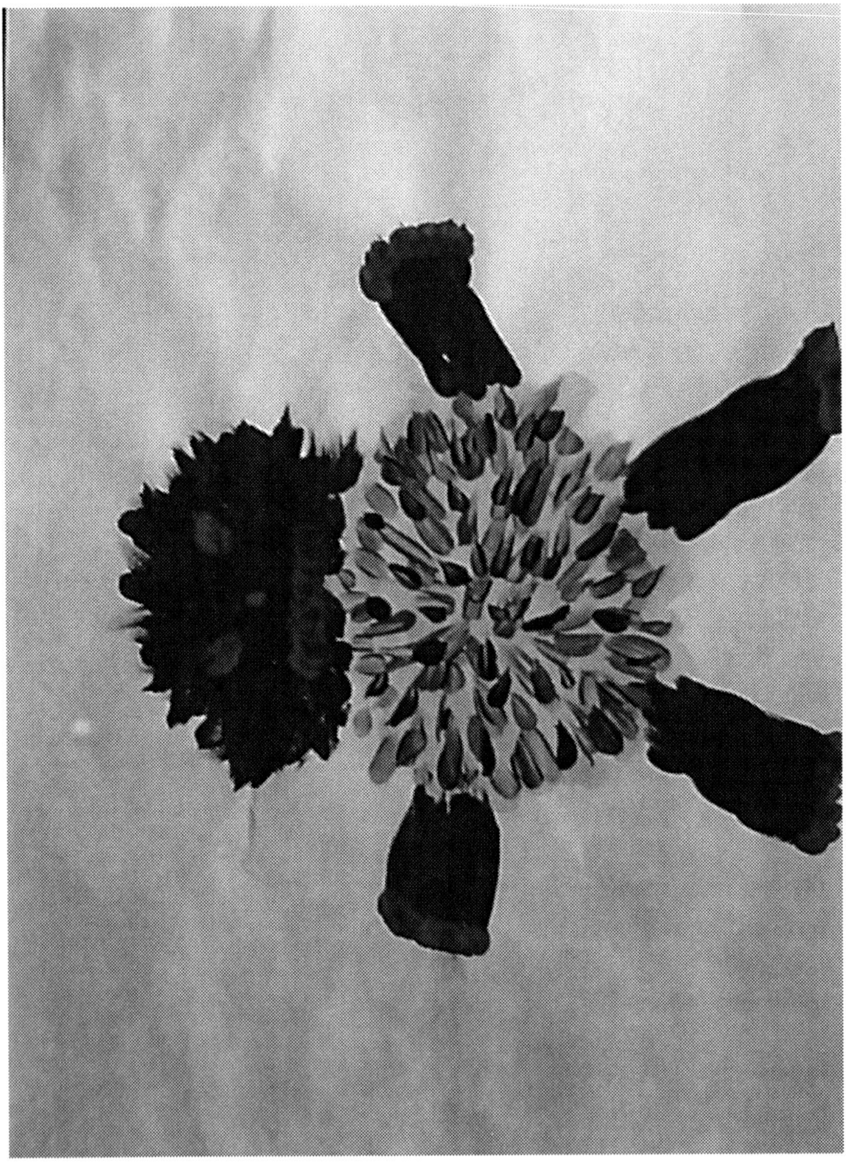

I Am Enough

My new job started off very well. I enjoyed treating patients and making new friends. This was an exciting time for me to be supporting myself. I felt I did well at challenging myself to develop a friend base of my own instead of isolating, which would have been my natural tendency.

Matt finished his student teaching in Australia. We had been able to keep our relationship going long-distance for quite some time. We were both ecstatic when he found a teaching job in the Chicago area. Finally, we could be together in person! He moved into an apartment just down the road from me. Life seemed to be going great. Life can also be deceiving.

* * *

About a year after I moved to Chicago, a friend of mine and I got the bug to train for the Chicago Marathon. We both thrive on new challenges, and October 9, 2000, became the latest one. Her husband and Matt eventually decided to train and run with us. So, we attacked the challenge as a foursome. I had always thought that running a marathon was something I wanted to do. I was so happy to have found people who wanted to do it with me. Running had always been something I loved to do, and I saw this as an opportunity to fall more in love with it.

I knew that this training would have me running distances far beyond those that I had ever run before, and I felt like I approached the training healthily. My eyes became open, however, to changes that I needed to make in my diet due to the increased physical demands I was placing on my body. After one twelve-mile training run one night along Chicago's beautiful lakeshore, Matt and I went back to his apartment to make dinner. As I stood at the counter cutting vegetables, I fainted. This was an obvious clue to me that my body wasn't getting what it needed.

I decided that I'd better have my diet checked out, so I visited a sports nutritionist. She analyzed my current eating habits and helped me see where I was deficient—namely in the areas of protein and fat. I took her suggestions and made the appropriate changes in my diet and successfully completed the marathon with Matt and our friends by my side. It was an incredible feeling of accomplishment—one I will never forget.

* * *

A few months after Matt moved to Chicago, he began facing a battle of his own—one with depression and anxiety. In essence, he became overloaded by the numerous life changes that had occurred in a relatively short period of time. He had spent some recent time in Australia to finish his student teaching, moved to Chicago, began a new and first job, and began seriously dating me. He came to realize that stress and life's challenges didn't roll off his back quite as easily as he thought they always had and would.

Matt's new job as a first-year teacher brought him new challenges. Perfectionism and higher expectations—these became part of Matt's world like he had never known before. His confidence became shaken. Depression set in, and the easy-going, happy-go-lucky Matt I had known before became clouded by confusion.

These unfortunate circumstances seemed to provide an opportunity for Matt and me to grow even closer. He told me that he needed me for support. It felt oftly good to be needed—probably too good. I wanted to take away his pain and make him see he was the wonderful and worthy man that I love and know. But no matter how hard I tried to make up for the confidence and self-love that he lacked inside, he was the only one who could truly give those gifts to himself.

To a certain degree, I was care-taking—a characteristic often common amongst people with eating disorders. I would often feel good about myself because I could help Matt feel better about himself at times. The problem came about when I *needed* to care-take to feel good about myself. I didn't like myself just for who I was.

Through various connections, we found a wonderful Christian counselor who began to give Matt skills and ways to combat his anxiety. He worked extremely hard to find himself again. Over the last couple of years, he has found success in dealing with his issues. The evolution of Matt Calvin continues, but today his journey seems filled with much more peace and contentment. I'm very proud of him.

* * *

I Am Enough

In March, 2000, one of the most amazing and wonderful moments of my life occurred. It was the moment that little girls everywhere dream of. A boy asked me to marry him. And not just any boy—the boy I'd had a crush on since junior high—Matt Calvin. It was like a dream come true to me. I can reflect upon an evening I spent with my sister in Kansas City a few years prior to this moment, during which she told me I had a choice—"either make Matt Calvin notice you or move on past your infatuation." I thank God that he finally caught on—slow as it was.

We were spending a weekend in Door County, Wisconsin, and he got down on his knee that Saturday afternoon and asked me to be his wife. I felt swept off my feet. I knew we were seriously moving in this direction because we had discussed it, but I didn't expect it to happen this particular weekend. I felt at peace. He was my soul mate, and the thoughts of what we could accomplish together flooded me. One of the best parts about it was that because of the work I had done in college with counseling, I knew that marriage wasn't something that I had to have to complete my life. My new journey with Matt would enhance the life I already had carved out for myself.

The next year and three months were filled with wedding planning. My journey with restriction during this time continued little by little. I would slowly cut back here and there—not in an unhealthy manner, but I was definitely being slowly pulled into the eating disorder cycle. Most of my "cutting back" was in preparation to look fabulous on my wedding day. Once the measurements for my dress had been taken, I certainly didn't want to gain any weight. Therefore, the options in my mind were to stay just as I was or lose a little.

Matt's fight with depression continued as did my need and desire to fill a care-taking role for him. We faced some rough times as far as doubting if what we were planning was right, but I believe that, in the end, these times of doubt helped solidify for us that marriage was the right step to take.

Our wedding weekend finally came! And unfortunately obsession about food came right along with it for me. I worried about whether or not I'd be able to allow myself to have fettuccini alfredo at the rehearsal dinner. I don't think I did. And I worried about someone else fixing my plate for me at our reception. I remember also worrying about letting myself order any dessert when Matt and I got back to the hotel. As much as I hate to admit it, my food obsessions really took off at this point in my life—this particular weekend.

We left on a wonderfully planned honeymoon to Ireland the Monday after our wedding. Despite our rental car being broken into and our belongings stolen, it should have been a relaxing vacation. In many ways it was. But my worries about food continued. I feared the Irish breakfasts and "pub food." And of course, I had to work out. The second marathon would come in October, and it was time to start training again.

* * *

Matt and I began the long weekend runs and carbo-loading again to train for our next Chicago Marathon. During this time, Matt continued to struggle with depression and anxiety. During our training for this marathon, my eating was somewhat more stabilized. I had learned more appropriate foods to eat and was able to avoid the fainting spells this time. The marathon came once again in October, and our time was fifteen minutes better than we had run during the first marathon. I must admit that a little of the excitement post-marathon had dwindled. It still felt awesome to finish and to have done better than the previous year, but it wasn't as thrilling as the first time. I didn't expect it to be, though.

As the new year rolled around, Matt seemed to be struggling even more with depression. I came to a point that I didn't know how to help him anymore. I was no longer able to be the consolation for him that I wanted to be, and I was struggling with how I was to be a support for him at this time. Our situation had changed now that we were married. I could no longer say to Matt, "I'll see you tomorrow," and go home to my own place if I became frustrated. I was now fully enmeshed in his moods and struggles. This is exactly where I wanted to be, but I needed some guidance on how to be in this position healthily, both for me and our marriage. Thus, I sought my own counseling.

I began seeing a therapist in January, 2002, to talk about my own struggles and frustrations in regard to Matt's depression. Since I'd been through successful counseling before I had hopes that this round would be no exception. I went once every couple of weeks and began to feel like I was gaining a healthy perspective on aspects of my own personality that I could change or improve so that I interacted with Matt on a healthier level. I really thought this was exactly what was happening. Now that I reflect back on it, I may have been realizing things that needed to change, but I had no idea how to begin changing them. Little did I realize that my own personal issues were just beginning to surface and that what was just ahead would be a much more dramatic situation than either Matt or I had ever found ourselves in the midst of before.

Chapter Six

"The Monster Within Me"

I want to restrict.
I want to feel empty.
What does this mean?
It's the monster within me.

I want to lash out.
In anger and rage.
Why is that so?
My monster is out of its cage.

I want to deprive
Myself of its needs.
How can I live
With this monster so mean?

I want to hurt me
But no one else.
How can this be?
This monster is hell.

I want to be numb.
And not feel a thing.
As long as I do
The monster won't sting.

9/13/03

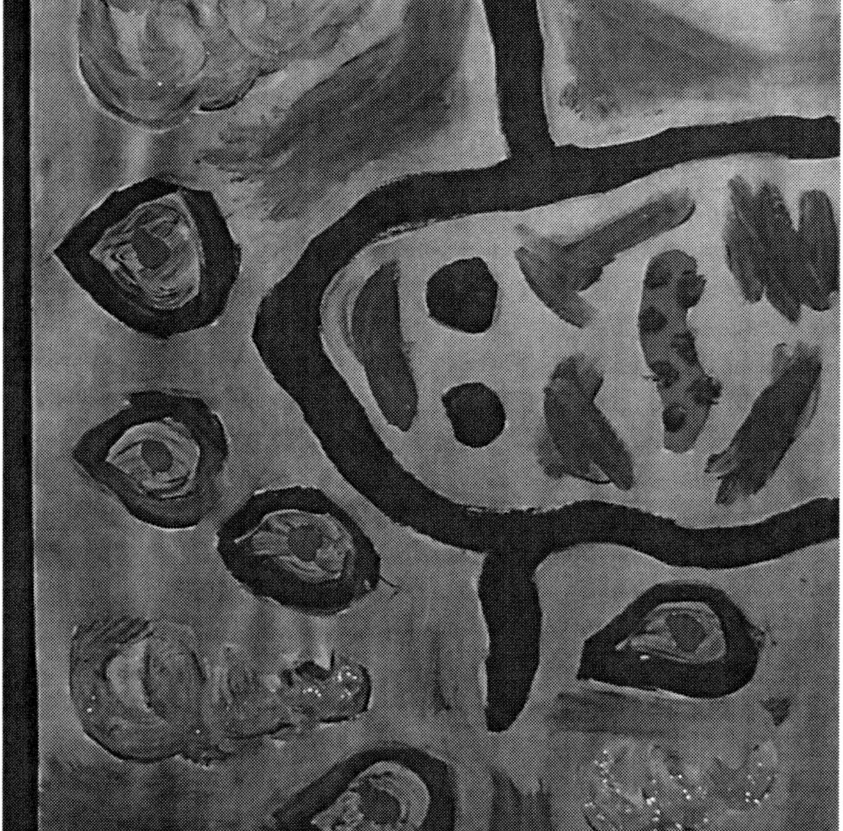

Shortly after the beginning of the new year, 2002, I remember saying offhandedly to one of my patients, "I am so damn hungry all the time." She looked back at me and responded, "Well you're not pregnant, are you?" My response of "Oh God, no" made me start to wonder exactly why I was so hungry if it wasn't that I was pregnant. Toward the end of my counseling in February, 2002, I remember telling the therapist a couple of different times that I felt like I was starting to worry excessively about what I was eating. In my eyes, she blew me off each time I got up enough courage to bring up the situation. It wasn't something I enjoyed discussing. It felt very much to me like my therapist was ready to be done with me. It was like she didn't even want to begin to tackle this issue with me. It only took a couple of times of her brushing me off regarding my food worries; I was ready to be done with her as well.

I decided that my worries were becoming great enough that I would seek out a nutritionist to visit once just to have her check out my current eating habits and offer any help she could. So, I called the local hospital and set up an appointment with one of their nutritionists.

Little did I know that when I left this appointment, my path down the eating disorder lifestyle would be solidified. I explained to the nutritionist that I had been worrying excessively about my food intake and felt as if I'd been slowly cutting back. She proceeded to tell me that, for my body type, I was taking in just the right amount of food and that, when I began training for the marathon again, I only needed to increase my food intake by three hundred calories! I was floored! I left the appointment feeling worse than when I showed up as I knew I was taking in too little food for me, but she told me just the opposite—that I was doing just fine.

I decided to give her suggestion a try and fit my food intake into the caloric number she gave me. To meet this goal, I had to cut back more than I already had. Thus, I came to feel that for all these years, I'd been overeating, even though my body had remained at its normal set point. This nutritionist had really given me poor advice, and I didn't know any better at this point than to trust her words. I still have significant anger concerning how she misled me, but underneath the anger is sadness for all the other people she may have misled as well.

I slowly became more and more frustrated as I tried to feel filled up on this too-small number of calories. I also became increasingly focused on food to the point that my breakfast and lunch were exactly the same every day, and the times at which I ate them were very regimented. I couldn't start either meal until my watch read a certain time, and I stretched each one as long as possible.

* * *

The interesting dynamic that began to play out in our marriage was that, as soon as Matt began to feel more in control of his depression, I began to feel more out of control regarding my food intake. It was as if we traded the role of "identified patient" from Matt to myself. Little did either of us realize at this time that what I was dealing with went far beyond what I could and couldn't eat. Our marriage seemed to need some kind of drama occurring in order for us to function.

Matt and I became increasingly distant from one another. It seemed as though we had unlearned how to communicate. I became more and more withdrawn as depression began to overtake me. I couldn't interact with Matt in the ways I wanted to—physically, emotionally, or spiritually. I withdrew from friends, and social outings, both individually and as a couple; it became something I feared. I felt like I didn't know how to interact with even my closest friends.

* * *

Our first anniversary rolled around on June 16, 2002. I had looked forward to and hoped this day would be one of the happiest Matt and I would have—just like one year prior. Unfortunately, it just so happened that we spent the day in a fight. The sadness of our interaction that day overtook me in the afternoon. I went to our bedroom, crawled up on our bed, and cried, and cried, and cried, curled up in the fetal position. I was crying for much more than that day, though. Never had I cried like I cried then, and never have I cried to that extent since. I sobbed. The sobs were for my pain as a child, for my mom and her pain, for the pain and exhaustion I'd endured over the last year trying to starve myself, for Matt and his pain, for the dissatisfaction both he and I felt in our marriage, for the fear of what lay ahead, and so, so much more. Matt crawled onto the bed and just wrapped his arms around me as I cried. We must have lain there for two hours. I didn't realize I'd had so many tears inside that needed to be released. I felt exhausted once they'd all been emptied.

This was my breaking point. I said out loud to both Matt and myself that I needed help. I could no longer live this way. Something had to change. I realized that my obsession with food had gotten completely out of control. I could not stop it on my own. Matt and I had a long talk about where to go from here. We decided that we would meet with our marriage counselor that next week and let her know of my true struggles in hopes that she would point us in the right direction to getting the help I needed. We did just that, and, very soon, I had set up initial appointments with a psychologist and a nutritionist.

Chapter Seven

"Confusion"

Where do I go?
Where do I turn?
What do I do
To heal this great burn?

Emotions are buried
Deep in my soul.
Where do I find them?
I'm out of control.

"Don't you give in!"
The voice inside speaks.
"You don't need food.
It's better to be weak."

"Your body is strong.
It needs no extra fuel.
Do what you want.
Be stubborn as a mule!"

I don't want to lose
My willpower so strong.
Though I can't live like this.
It's just all wrong.

9/13/03

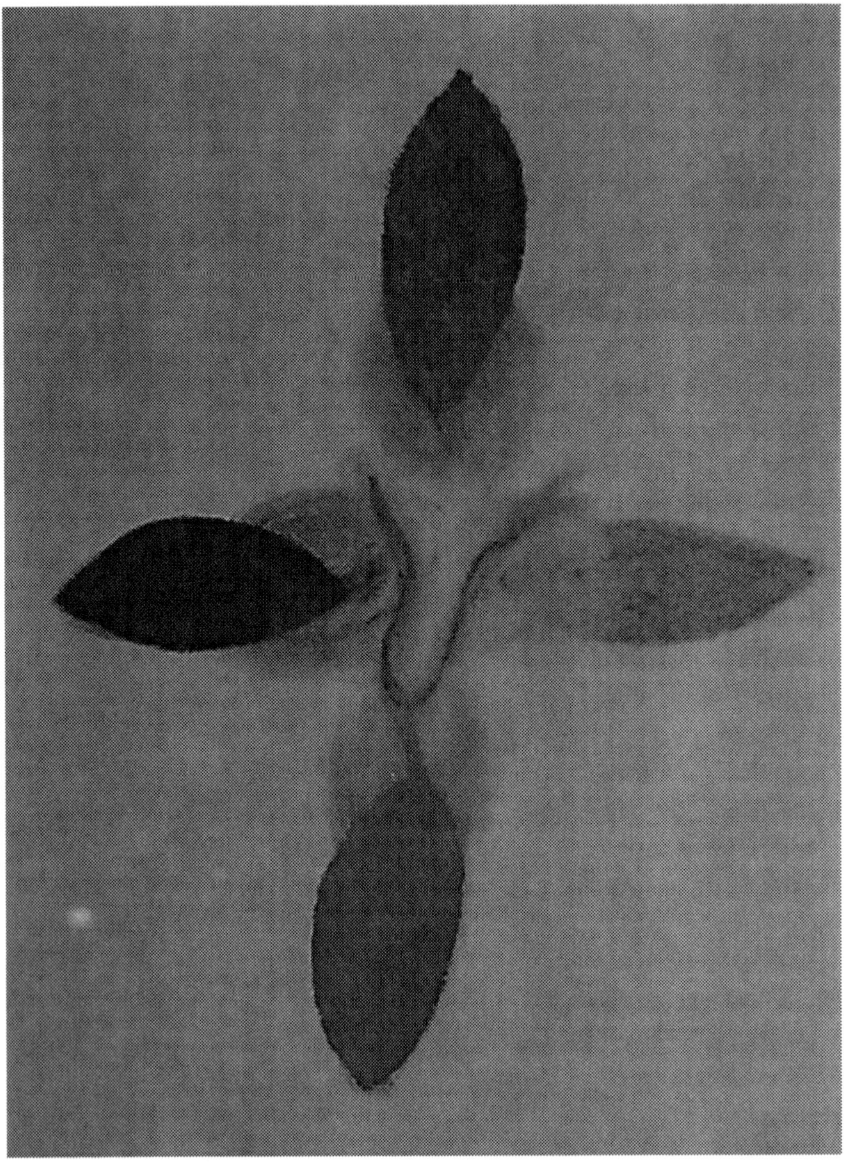

I remember feeling very confused at this time about all that was beginning to surface and take shape. I was afraid of admitting my fears and terrified of what I was facing now, but I knew I couldn't keep putting me and Matt through this torture. I think that in my heart, I knew I needed help for myself, but my motivation for seeking the counseling was to improve our marriage. My motives would need to shift in order to truly begin to make any changes.

I was frightened but also relieved to have my first visit with my nutritionist. I was nervous about what I would hear because of my previous experience with a nutritionist. But I was also eager to voice my struggles. I feared, though, that they might not be valid struggles or that I would walk into her office and hear her say to me, "You're overreacting. You don't need to be here." Once I started revealing my worries, I was relieved, in a way, to hear her say just the opposite to me. I remember her eyes seeming ready to pop out of her head from disbelief as I told her what the other nutritionist had advised me to do. I was also honest about my starting to train again for my third marathon. I remember leaving her office feeling like I had permission to eat again. She assured me she would work closely with me and wouldn't let me "blow up" once I began eating more. Black and white thinking had been my thought process for quite some time. I faced it in this case as well. I feared that if I increased my food intake at all, I would go completely to the other extreme and gain enormous amounts of weight because I would lose control and not be able to restrain myself. I was just beginning to realize that I had already seriously begun to lose control of my food intake, and the food was now controlling me and my life. I wanted to trust my nutritionist and believe what she told me.

She confirmed for me that I was really in a danger zone. I was essentially sitting on a fence and could fall either way at this point. I think I really did feel some relief that I could do such things as re-institute bagels into my diet—a fear food for me that I had cut out some time before. She helped me to begin to understand just what I would need to do in order to nourish my body properly while training for the marathon. I felt like I was in good hands. I would just have to trust her and try to reach the goals I set with her.

Despite the fact that I was now in treatment, it continued to get harder and harder to make myself stick to my food plan. I kept wanting to cut back little by little. And my marathon training kept increasing little by little. The combination of the two was not healthy.

***

My social skills seemed to be declining by the day. Matt and I returned home to Kansas City in July for Karyn's wedding. I remember feeling extremely out of place and self-conscious around even family. My discomfort with food and people seemed very apparent to me and probably to others who were around me.

I continued training, and the marathon came again for the third time. I was very lucky that I was even able to contemplate running it. I had not nourished myself properly, and I know that Matt, my family, and my therapists were glad when it was over and I had come through it safely. My training friends and I had run our slowest time. I was disappointed, and the feeling of satisfaction that I'd felt the previous two years was absent this time. I wasn't sure why I had run it. I think I felt like it was the thing I "should" do. Matt's philosophy was, "I ran it once to prove I could do it, a second time to prove I was stupid, and I feel no need to run it a third time." Needless to say, he didn't run it with me the third time.

This marathon was a turning point for me. Yes, I had used it as an excuse to lose some weight, but I had managed to keep myself nourished enough that I safely made it through the race. Inside, though, I freaked out when it was over because my way of purging would significantly decrease now. I would no longer be running those excessively long distances. I was told it would be best if I took a year off of racing so that I could get healthier. That scared me to death. I tremendously feared backing off of running for fear of gaining weight. Thus, I began a more deliberate cut-back on food.

A change had occurred. I was now making a much more conscious choice to not eat than I had before. I began depleting myself enough that I was isolating from virtually everyone, Matt included. I was completely obsessed with food. My concentration suffered. I was exhausted, hated working out but felt like I should anyway, and only wanted to sleep. I became stagnant with my therapy and was told to go home a couple of different times because my focus and concentration were so poor that I wouldn't get anything out of the session. Something had to change. I had reached another breaking point.

Still, I wasn't yet ready to get better. In fact, I wanted to get sicker in many ways. I knew I was wasting my time and my therapists' time because I was making no progress. I felt bad using up their appointments when I knew I would leave their offices with no intention of taking their suggestions or working toward making any goals to progress healthily. I also knew that if I stayed on my current course, I was going to get nothing but worse and probably end up in a hospital. At this point, I didn't really care what happened to me or what I did to myself, but I didn't want to put Matt or our marriage through anything more devastating. It's difficult to explain the tug of war and ambivalence that were going on inside of me.

On some level, I wanted to stop this madness and start to turn it around because I was willing to let go of my eating disorder. However, it still served many purposes for me, and I was terrified to think of living without it.

Chapter Eight

"Punishment"

I want some boxing gloves
To bruise my stomach up.
I want to hit and pound it
And beat it to a pulp.

My need for punishment
Is strong in every way:
To starve myself, to exercise,
And waste myself away.

I want to punch my stomach hard
And hit my forehead, too.
I feel as though I don't deserve
To feel anything other than blue.

I need to put the bat away
And stop beating myself up.
I'm feeling bruised and battered
And all broken up.

9/21/03

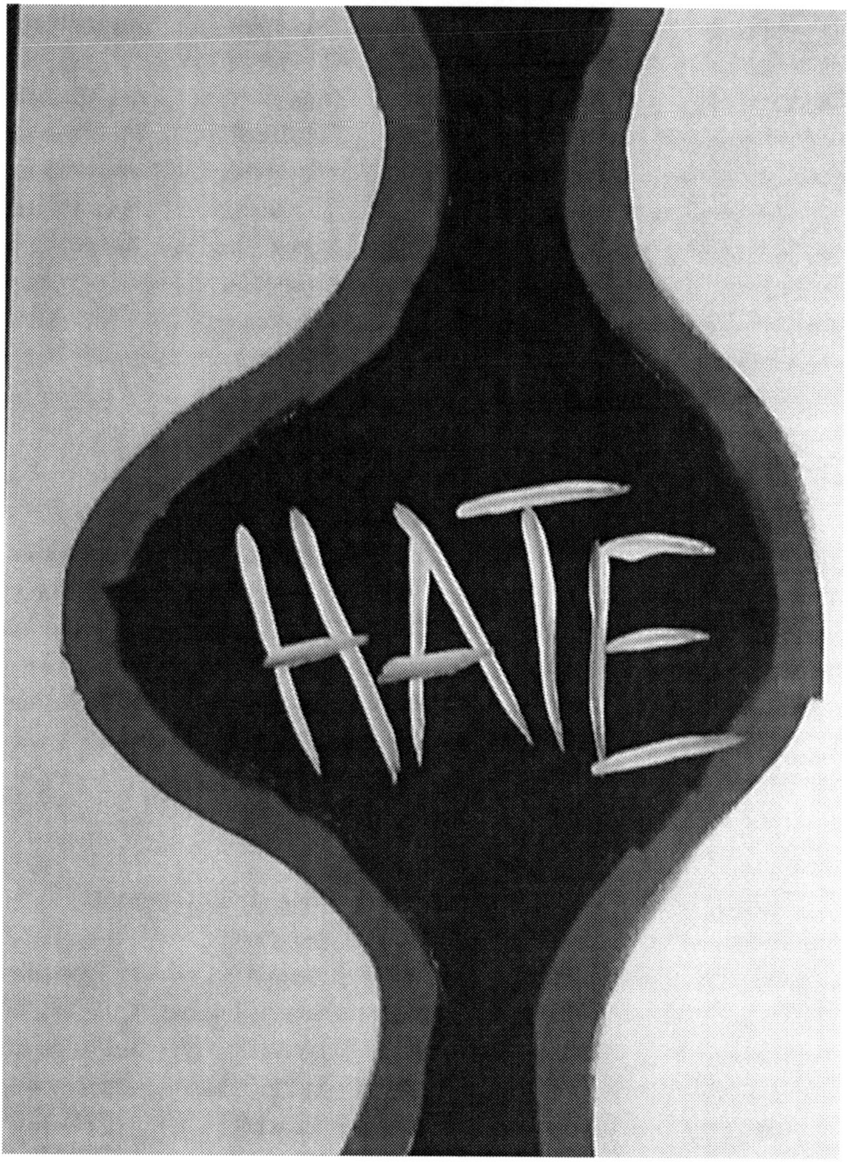
HATE

The Thanksgiving after Karyn's wedding was difficult for me. Matt and I drove home to spend the day with his immediate and extended family. I remember feeling so frightened to spend an entire day with people I didn't feel like I knew very well. Matt and I sat in a parking lot down the street from his parents' house while I cried. I didn't want to be teary around his family. Matt's parents knew my situation, but the rest of the family did not know at the time. So there I was, playing the hiding game once again. I was terrified of sharing my emotions, so I put on my happy face and tried to act like there was nothing wrong.

The food buffet scared me to death. I participated some in the activities going on, but I mostly isolated myself for fear that no one wanted me there. I felt horrible about the way I acted because Matt was looking so forward to spending time with his family. I felt like I couldn't be a part of it. I left him alone and even isolated myself from him because I feared I would ruin his time.

* * *

The time from Christmas of that year through the spring of the next year is very spotty in my mind. I don't honestly remember much of what went on. Part of that, I believe, is because I just was not present in my interactions with others. My mind was clouded from restriction. I was isolating myself as much as possible and was very into my eating disorder. I remember just floating through the days without doing much other than paying attention to my eating disorder. It was my world.

* * *

In early June, I was in my therapist's office, energy-depleted from restricting. I was too tired to really participate in much therapy. I had been restricting more and more. That night, my therapist told me that she thought something a little more drastic needed to be implemented to try and curb my restriction. We settled on asking my mom to come stay with Matt and me and prepare my meals. Eating dinner was becoming particularly difficult for me. My therapist thought it would be helpful for Mom to make dinner and have it ready when I walked in the door, coming home from work. Eating dinner would be the first thing I would do.

I Am Enough

So we called my mom right then and there and asked her if she'd be willing to come. She never hesitated and said she'd be there as soon as we needed her to be there. She came on a Saturday night and stayed through the next week. She met me at work and ate lunch with me. We talked and talked and talked. I craved talking with her about what I was feeling and why I felt I needed to keep restricting.

Mom talked to my nutritionist to plan dinners that would have the exchanges I needed. She would sit and eat dinner with Matt and me. Conversation was easier with three people, and my focus was diverted some from what I was eating if there was more conversation. Mom's purpose in coming was not to be the food police. She simply cooked the food, but I still had the choice of whether or not I would eat it.

Yes, Matt could have fulfilled the same role and made all the food, but my therapist and I felt it would be better for my relationship with Matt if he was taken out of the equation. My tendency would be to get angry with the person cooking the food, and, right now, it was better that I get angry at Mom than at Matt.

More than anything, it was so comforting to have Mom around for an extended period of time. I could talk to her easily, and she really listened to me. I was thankful for her companionship. Her visit served its purpose as I ate more than I would have had she not come. But I knew that, when she left, I would go right back to restricting as I had before she left. What would it take to stop my spiral?

The day after Mom left, Matt and I traveled to Playa del Carmen, Mexico, for a week-long vacation. My treatment team was not thrilled about my going. I was lucky to be given the go-ahead. I made a contract with my nutritionist that I would eat every three to four hours and that I would exercise no more than three days. I didn't keep the contract and continued to restrict on the trip. Matt and I had arguments about it. He knew what I was doing. I had looked so forward to going, but the trip ended up not being as relaxing as I'd hoped. I continued to have a difficult time with intimacy. We had a nice time, but it could have been much more enjoyable had we not been dealing with these issues.

Chapter Nine

"Hunger"

Hunger—
What is it?
I really don't know.

Hunger—
What does it feel like?
I used to know.

Hunger—
How do I find it?
Will I ever know?

Hunger—
I fear it.
It scares me to death.

Hunger—Hunger—Hunger—Hunger

9/15/03

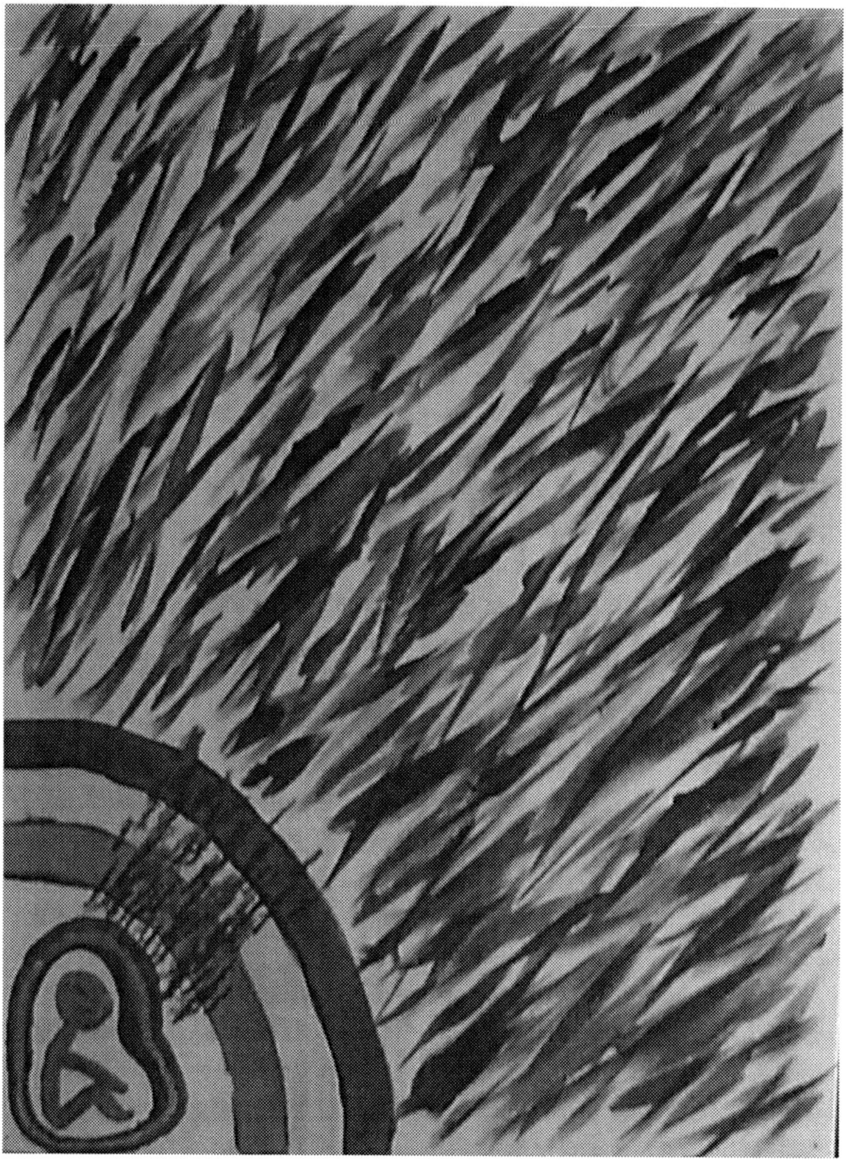

The lack of clarity that I felt from January to June reinforced my growing awareness of a need for help. In order to begin any kind of road to recovery, I knew that I needed to remove myself from my environment. I needed a new place to gain some perspective. I also knew I needed to take this time for myself, but I definitely felt guilty about it. I felt guilt about taking time off from my job and about leaving Matt for this time. I knew, though, that in order to be able to truly work on fighting my eating disorder, I needed to immerse myself in daily treatment. The option I chose as far as treatment was to enter a residential treatment program in Philadelphia called The Renfrew Center. It definitely turned out to be the best treatment choice.

After working through much stress with insurance companies and treatment facilities, I was accepted into Renfrew's program. Thankfully, I qualified for and was able to take medical leave from my job. I was blessed to have an employer who agreed that my health had to come first. Matt and I packed my stuff in our car and set off for the drive from Chicago to Philadelphia. It was definitely a long trip, but we were both so happy that we had that time together as we would be apart for at least the next three weeks. It was a beautiful drive, and I believe it helped me to sort out some of my emotions and get more used to the idea of what I was about to start.

* * *

We arrived in Philadelphia on a Wednesday, and I was to check in on Thursday. Insurance issues arose, and I ended up not checking in until Friday. So, Matt and I took advantage of the extra day and took the train into New York. Matt had never been to Manhattan before, so we hiked all over the town that day and enjoyed some surprisingly relaxed time together.

My first day at Renfrew brought tears similar to the day of our first anniversary. I surprised myself at how weepy I became. My emotions had felt so locked up inside for the longest time and I hadn't known what it would take to get me to cry again. Obviously, this was it. I cried out of fear, because I would be apart from my husband for an extended time, because I was going to have to eat, because I wasn't going to be able to work out, because I was going to face issues I'd never faced before and many, many more reasons. It was a day like I'd never experienced.

My first lunch consisted of tofu, which I had never tasted before. I didn't even know what it was when the lid to my plate was lifted. Surprisingly, I developed a strong liking for it during my time at Renfrew. From my first day on at Renfrew, I felt permission to eat there. I hadn't felt that in quite some time. The support at mealtime was incredible. I felt immediately accepted by the other women as they urged me on to finish my meals.

Overwhelming is how I would describe my first day at Renfrew. I met so many new people and had no idea how I'd keep everything straight. Everyone I came into contact with made me feel accepted like I'd never felt before. It was okay to cry and show my emotions. I didn't get stared at or made fun of even though I felt weak for crying. The day ended with Matt and me sitting in on a family group meeting. I felt so supported having him next to me. My emotions and fear were running high, but he calmed them in a way by letting me know he was supporting me one-hundred percent.

The time came to say goodbye to Matt. At that time, we expected my stay to be twenty-one days, and we weren't sure if he would come visit or not. I knew I needed time to myself, but I didn't want to watch him go. He gave me confidence that I had made the right decision. He kissed my forehead and watched me walk inside before he left. I missed him already.

* * *

The next day started early with a 5:15 AM vital check. I knew this would be another hard day. I wondered how Matt was after such a long and tiring experience the day before. I wanted to call my parents already but knew I should wait. I needed to learn how to support myself a bit. After one of my groups, I found that Matt had left me a plant for my room and the fourth Harry Potter book to read during my down time. I actually had a few minutes to see him once again before he took off for the airport. It was difficult, but I'm so glad we connected one last time.

I remember feeling that the second day was all about food for me. I was extremely worried about the amount I was eating—as was everyone. I felt uncomfortably full as I hadn't had this much food in my stomach for quite some time. My solace that day was in a girl who had checked in with me the day before. We immediately connected when we found out we were both Christians. It was so wonderful to find out that I shared that with someone there. I was grateful for her positive outlook that day.

By the end of the weekend, I was really wondering why I was eating. I knew it wasn't for myself. It felt like I was eating because of the encouragement of the others. I didn't want to let them down by not finishing. Plus, it still felt easier to eat at Renfrew than it did at home. I was starting to feel more comfortable there overall.

From day one, I learned that care-taking for the other women was not allowed. Points could be accrued against a patient if she were caught playing a care-taking role. I was so used to care-taking for Mom, Dad, Matt, and many others; I knew I would have to be careful and watch my involvement with others. Later on in my stay at Renfrew, I was tempted often to care-take for the newer patients. I knew their anxiety, frustrations, and pain, and I so desperately wanted to take it all away.

* * *

I had developed a definite exercise addiction that I knew I needed to deal with. So, I decided I would be pro-active, and I met with the exercise coordinator to talk about my struggles. My urges to exercise were high, and it was helpful to process with her why I was abusing my body with exercise. She told me that I could enter the exercise program the following week as long as my body remained stabilized.

I craved the groups and counseling. I needed to talk about my present situation concerning everything, and these people would listen! They wanted to know more, and I hadn't felt that from strangers before. It was as if they cared about me simply because I was a human. I felt a unique connection with these counselors and women. It was as if our eating disorders made us sisters. There was unconditional acceptance. This is not how it was on "the outside." We were in a safe bubble, and I never wanted to leave.

I became very aware that I had lost my mind-body connection. The loss felt severe. I felt completely disconnected and had no idea how I would regain that connection. I remember the first time I felt peace within again. It was during one of my relaxation groups, and it felt amazing. It felt like a small heaven on earth. I came away from the meditation not feeling sleepy or sluggish but more centered and focused. I wondered, however, if it was just a fluke or if I would be able to feel that again.

One of my greatest challenges came during that first week. My counselor challenged me to sit with myself for an hour a day (an eternity to me) and let thoughts come to my mind of who I am, what I want, what I need, what I believe, etc. I knew I couldn't participate fully in my marriage if I didn't know myself. This was one way I could start to get acquainted. I feared the challenge as I feared Matt being disappointed if I found out I was a different person than he thought I was. I think I feared even more, though, that I might personally not be satisfied with my true self. However, it was a risk I had to take.

I began to journal on my first day at Renfrew, wanting to keep a record of my thoughts during my stay there. I had never enjoyed writing before, but the words seemed to come easily at this stage. I needed a place to sort out all the feelings I was experiencing, and the journal provided that for me. I wrote multiple times daily. It helped to calm me when I felt anxious. It became my daily dialogue with myself.

As my first week at Renfrew came to a close, I reflected back on what I had accomplished. I began to re-initiate my mind-body connection, challenged myself not to isolate, began to discover "who I am," understood I need to pay attention to my needs, realized that I needed to make changes in my daily routine when I returned home, and realized also that Renfrew was where I needed to be at that time.

Chapter Ten

"Punishment"

I'm angry.
I'm mad.
I'm frustrated.
I'm sad.

I don't want to eat.
I just want to sleep.
I don't want to move—
Just lie in a heap.

I feel I should run.
I feel I should sweat.
I feel I should burn
Myself in this heat.

I just want to punch
Myself in the gut.
I feel like I'm stuck,
Deep in this rut.

I want to feel pain
And punishment, too.
It makes me feel good
To hurt through and through.

9/13/03

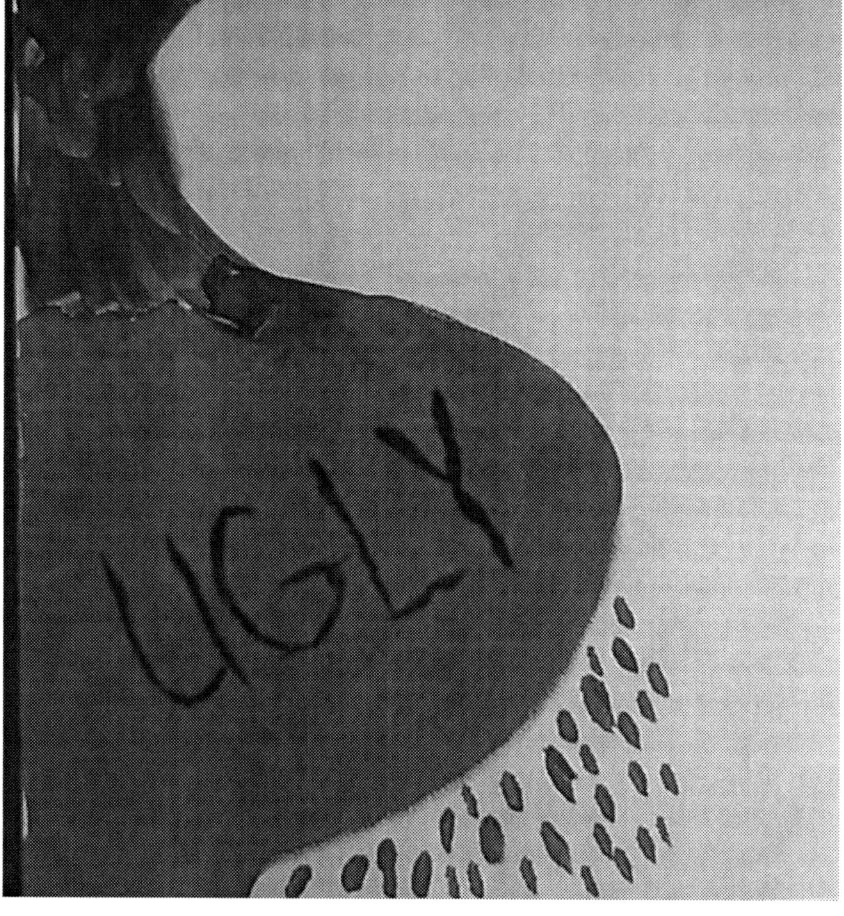
UGLY

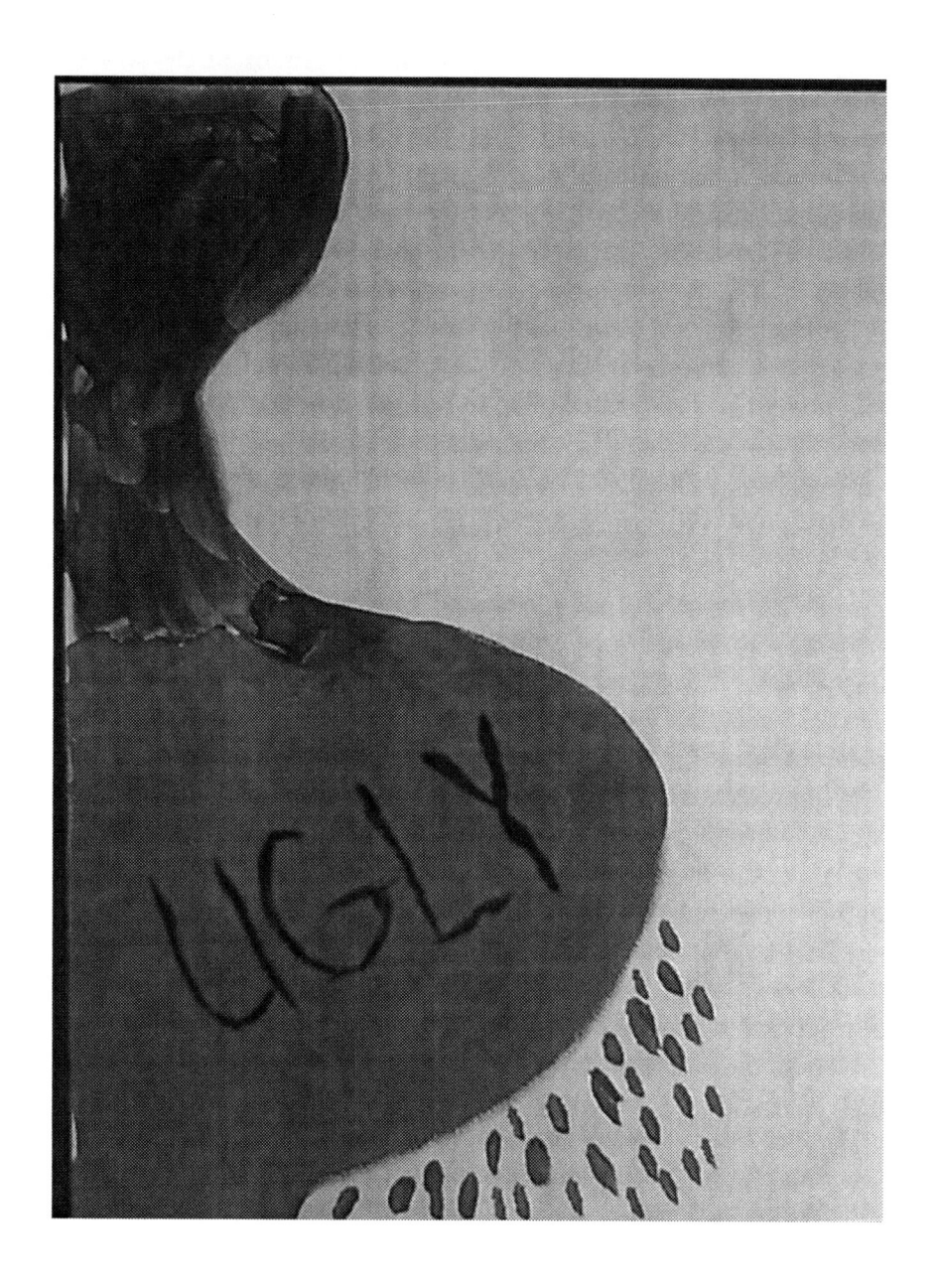

The first time I went to exercise group, I came away feeling good about myself. Unlike my workouts before I went into Renfrew, I felt some energy afterward. We did a light workout compared to the long runs that I'd been forcing myself to do. I used muscles in ways they hadn't been used in a long time. I discovered that my body had become purely conditioned to running. At Renfrew, I was exposed to the idea that someone who is truly "in shape" is a person who has some cardiovascular endurance, a good strength base, and solid balance. I suddenly began to desire those components of being "in shape." I had the endurance, but that was about it.

Although I felt some positive energy from that first workout, I could not ignore the fact that I felt like I should do more. The guilt set in. Now that I had been allowed to resume some exercise, I needed to take it to the extreme. The important part is that I acknowledged that. I brought my guilt up to others and talked about it to gain support.

* * *

Matt came to visit me the second weekend I was in Renfrew. It felt very natural to be with him—much more so than it had felt in a long time. I felt more like my old self with him. I laughed, joked around some, and had so much to tell him. It felt refreshing to have conversation to offer. I hadn't felt like engaging with anyone in that way in quite a while. I felt present. It was great to just talk with him about progress I'd made, goals I still had, and my fears about returning home. Matt was so open with me and listened so attentively. I felt so blessed to have his incredible support.

During that next week, I continued to struggle with wanting to restrict and feeling like I should exercise. I struggled with finding the brainpower to be positive with my thoughts. I was frustrated because I didn't feel ready to give up my anorexia. I felt like I needed it; I wanted it.

I progressed through the meal plans like a "good girl." But I felt like I was eating for the program—not for myself.

I began to do some good work through my counseling sessions. I worked very hard at being as open as I could with my therapist. She and I began to develop a bond that I came to trust greatly. I would write her a note at the end of each day to explain how my day had gone,

I Am Enough

what struggles I had faced, feelings I had dealt with. I would then slip them under her office door each night. I really looked forward to writing my notes to her. Writing is a way that I can more easily express my thoughts, so it gave her more insight concerning me as a person, as well. It helped me gather my thoughts at the end of each day, too.

I tried to take time for myself to "just be." It was very uncomfortable at first to just sit still and be with my own mind and thoughts. I made lists of things I need, things I want, things I know, things I fear, reasons to recover, reasons not to recover. This started to give me some insight into myself, and they are lists I can return to as often as I would like.

* * *

I faced a very difficult personal challenge during my second week in Renfrew. I never wanted to know my actual weight, even before food became an issue for me. My mother had been obsessed for years about her weight. I saw her pain, anguish, elation, or disappointment after weighing herself. Her day seemed to be made or broken by what the scale read. I was terrified of developing the same obsession. Thus, I avoided weighing myself all together.

Even once I became overtaken by my eating disorder, I still did not want to know my weight. When I entered Renfrew, being weighed daily was a very scary thing to me. Each time, I stood with my back to the scale, being weighed blindly. The nurses and counselors agreed not to tell me my weight until my nutritionist began to feel that I was avoiding certain feelings by not looking at my weight. She felt that with all the support I had surrounding me at Renfrew, it would be healthier for me to find out my weight while there instead of in a more triggering way once I left Renfrew.

I thought about it and discussed it with my therapist and agreed that it would be a healthy thing for me to do. I was terrified a couple of days before I was to learn my weight. Would I be able to handle knowing? I didn't know how I would react or respond.

The fateful morning came, and I asked the nurses what the scale read. The number surprised me greatly as it was much lower than I had expected. The sad part about the disorder is that hearing that my weight was as low as it was made me happy. I came away from the experience feeling just the opposite of how I thought I would feel. Even though

I was relieved to a point, I experienced many other feelings as well. I had gained a small amount of weight in my two weeks at Renfrew, and I was frustrated at that. I was fearful that I would view more weight gain as failure and that I would now obsess about my weight. I felt sadness and frustration that these negative eating disorder thoughts were keeping me unhealthy. I felt a loss of self-control that I hadn't been able to exercise and relief, in a way, that my eating disordered thoughts hadn't left me. I was frustrated that my weight wasn't as low as many of the other girls and fearful that I would let myself continue to be defined by that number.

**

An assignment in one of my groups was to write a letter to someone or something relating to loss in my life. The three points we were to address were appreciation, resentment, and regret. I chose to write to my eating disorder. While writing this letter, I began to really see my ambivalence emerge. I saw the appreciation for my eating disorder quite easily. It provided me with a sense of comfort, control, and security (though false) when I felt like I had lost these. It provided me with a coping mechanism when I could find no other. Believe it or not, anorexia has given me some gifts. It has allowed my family relationships to grow and be strengthened. It has given me insight into my and my family's past. It has given me wisdom to see others for the people they are instead of just focusing on their outer shells. It has also provided a window to my true self.

However, I found that I harbor much resentment toward my eating disorder as well. It took away my emotions and my desire for connection with myself and others. It took away my self-confidence and enjoyment of life. It left me with emptiness.

Regret included the time the anorexia has taken away from me, my husband, and our new marriage. We had looked forward to having much more fun in the short two years we'd been married. I regret the doubtfulness and undue stress it's caused in my life. I regret the pain anorexia caused my mom.

The frustration and confusion surrounding this illness caused me to question how I can hate anorexia and its destructiveness so much yet love it, desire it, and yearn for its restrictiveness to be in my life. It's a pure addiction.

* * *

My parents came to visit the next weekend. I was so very glad that they took the time and money to see me in this environment and understand what I was working on. They came to a family therapy session with me and listened so openly as I confronted them with some feelings that I'd been dealing with regarding them and our past. I am very blessed to have them as parents. They listened with loving ears and responded openly, which fostered honesty. It was a positive experience. I felt proud to have them with me.

I ate out away from Renfrew for the first time with them. It felt very odd to be eating out in the regular world again. The menu looked absolutely overwhelming as I had gotten very used to picking from only two options. The restaurant was noisy, and I missed the companionship of the other girls. Altogether, I did fairly well with my meal. I believe it was a success even though I didn't want to view it as that.

I continued struggling with body image. My attention always gravitated toward my stomach. To me (and society), a flat stomach indicates strength, willpower, and success. If I didn't see a flat stomach in the mirror, I felt worthless and like a failure. I came to learn that I projected certain feelings inside myself onto my stomach. I felt fear of showing myself to others because I wouldn't be "enough." I had a fear of making my voice heard because I didn't want to bother others. I believed others' feelings should come first and that I'm not worthy enough to take care of myself. It was easier to hate my stomach than deal with my core feelings and beliefs.

My second week at Renfrew brought many worthwhile accomplishments, although it was hard for me to acknowledge them as that.

* * *

I'd never thought of myself as being very creative. Thus, when I learned that I would be going to art class as one of my sessions, I began to worry. I was concerned that I wouldn't be able to think of ideas to

Jennifer D. Calvin

use and that my art would be so much worse than everyone else's. I decided, though, that I would take a risk and give it a chance.

I began to feel at ease when I realized that other patients had the same fears I did. I surprised myself when I came up with responses to the assignment presented. The images seemed to come fairly easily to me. It was strange, but fulfilling, to see my thoughts drawn out before me. As that first session ended, I felt a sense of pride in myself that I had ventured out of my comfort zone and tried something new.

I started looking forward to going to art class. I could take whatever I made with me, and it became such a wonderful way for me to chart my progress. I was eager to show and explain my art to others. I found I could express my thoughts and feelings through art in ways that I had never experienced before. It became a way for me to express myself without having to talk. The time during which I worked on my art became a time of reflection and peace. I was alone with my thoughts. I was eager to see what my mind would come up with.

At first, my art felt somewhat forced, but I soon learned how to let my mind go wherever it wanted to go and allow my hands to follow in response. I came to enjoy and feel comfortable with painting the most. The feel of the brush on the canvas was soothing to me. Feeling this comfort was so wonderful for my type-A personality. It was hard for me to always accept my finished product as being right just how it was. I naturally worked for perfection and became frustrated with its flaws. The art therapist would remind us that flaws make the art unique and that it was expression, not perfection, for which we were working.

Chapter Eleven

"Why"

Why am I recovering when I'm not sure I really want to?
Do I?
I don't know.
I must
Because I am.

Do I have to?
No.
Well, yes—if I want to live.
Do I want to live?
I think I do,
But there is slight doubt.

What does recovering mean?
Feeling better.
Do I want that?
I fear it.
Why?
It's foreign.
It entails giving myself a gift.

Why do I want to punish myself?
It's easier.
Do I deserve to feel good?
Everyone else says I do.
I hate my stomach.
I want to lose weight.

Do I want to slip?
Yes—at times.
I don't want to recover perfectly.
I want to struggle.
I've striven for perfection too much already.
I don't need to recover perfectly.

What's behind all this?
I don't know.
My brain is tired.
I'm not perfect.
I think I like that.
Do I like myself?
Whoa—don't go there yet!

Why am I eating?
I have no clue.
Probably because I'm supposed to.
It's not for myself.
I still want to rebel.
I don't have to do anything I don't want to.

I've asked for and sought out help.
Does this mean that in some way I want to recover?
It must.
But why?

10/10/03

BUBBLE
PERSPECTIVE
ACCEPTANCE
CHALLENGE
NOURISHMENT
GROWTH
STRENGTH
LOVE
VOICE
REST

Matt and I had talked about his coming to visit again at the end of my third week, but as the time approached, I really started to feel like I needed a weekend to myself. I was extremely nervous and guilt-ridden about talking to Matt about this. It was an opportunity for me to use my voice and listen to what I needed for myself. So I took the risk and told Matt how I was feeling. He was so wonderful about it all. He seemed completely understanding of my need to use the time by myself. Of course, his response didn't take away my guilt over asking him not to come, but using my voice was a step in the right direction.

* * *

The most powerful therapy session I had during my time at Renfrew occurred during this third week. It was called a structured eating session. My therapist asked me to give her a list of three fear foods of mine, and she would pick one to bring in, and we would have a therapy session specifically around that food. I wasn't too sure about this initially, but as I think about it now, it was an amazing session. I chose as my fear food a Hershey's Cookies & Cream bar. Dessert foods were definitely fear foods for me. To start, my therapist took the candy bar out of her drawer and just set it on her desk. We talked about what feelings were coming up for me, and she gradually moved the candy bar towards me. In the meantime, she also had the same candy bar for herself, and she began to eat it. I had the option of eating or not eating mine. I finally held the candy bar as we continued to talk. It was amazing how I gradually became angry at the candy bar—or so it seemed. I definitely was projecting my anger onto the candy bar just as I'd been projecting so many other feelings onto food. I felt my anger and frustration build as well as my heartbeat. At the end of the session, my therapist asked me what I wanted to do with the candy bar. My eating disorder side wanted to chuck it into the trash. If the window had been open, I might have thrown it out. Instead, I placed it safely on top of a pillow. I believe my small rational side made that choice, and I believe that my decision to place it on the pillow was to show respect for that rationality even though my eating disordered side felt much stronger.

One of the main threads in the session seemed to be purpose: purpose of the food, purpose of my eating disorder, purpose of my life, and purpose of me as an individual. I feel like everything I do should serve some sort of purpose that does not include the purpose of enjoyment. In many ways, the eating disorder is a form of self-punishment.

I was struck at how I had more desire to eat the candy bar when it was first shown to me than I did by the end of the session. My anger at the candy bar definitely seemed to increase as the session went on.

I've always seemed to struggle with showing my emotions to others. The eating disorder definitely seemed to dull my emotions. During my stay at Renfrew and definitely before I went there, I'd not felt able to access any real emotions. I think I'd developed the belief that showing emotions is a weakness while holding them inside is a strength. This idea became another thread in the session. I was amazed at how my therapist was able to sit in the session and so easily, effortlessly, and seemingly quickly eat her candy bar. I felt empowered over her in one respect because I was able to resist mine. I saw myself on one level as having more willpower than her. I could parallel this with my thoughts that those who show their emotions (those who eat the candy bar) are weak, while those who restrain their emotions (those who resist the candy bar) are strong. Rationally, I know the reverse is true.

* * *

As my third week came to an end, I still felt like I hadn't accessed many of my true feelings. That had been extremely frustrating to me. I felt ready to show my emotions, but they weren't coming up for me to be able to let them out. I still felt numb.

My original stay of twenty-one days became extended to include two more weeks. This decision was made by myself and my treatment team together. I was very thankful for the extension as I felt I could really benefit from more time there. I was very blessed to have insurance that did not fight the need for an extension.

* * *

At the end of my fourth week, I transitioned out of the residential program and into the day program. The first part of the week, I really began to focus on my feelings regarding the days after the completion of Renfrew's program and my return home. I had a family therapy session with Matt to discuss my concerns. Once again, he was very willing and eager to work with me. One of my main concerns was that, when I returned home, Matt and I would revert back to poor communication. I was also concerned about this potential view: "Jen was the one who went away to do the work, so all the changes need to come from her." I needed us both to take responsibility for our relationship. Matt had been doing his own counseling in my absence, so my hope was that he was feeling more secure in his role. From my perspective, I needed him to take responsibility and ownership for his own feelings, reactions, and emotions. I knew my part of the bargain would be to be direct and clear about my needs. If I felt like being overly quiet and withdrawn, I needed to look inside myself to see if I had any fears or emotions that I might be stuffing down.

Chapter Twelve

"I Should"

I know what I should do.
Does this mean I should do it?
I don't know.
Is what I should do what I want to do?
I'm not sure yet.

I think I want to restrict.
Is restricting what I should do?
Not if I want to recover.
Do I want to recover?
Maybe. Probably. I don't know.

What if I really don't want to restrict?
That really scares me.
I want to want to restrict.
I don't want to want to eat.

Is recovery failure?
Of course not—rationally.
In some ways, it seems like failure to me.
Can I live without an eating disorder?
I'm sure I could.
Do I want to?
The jury is still out.

10/10/03

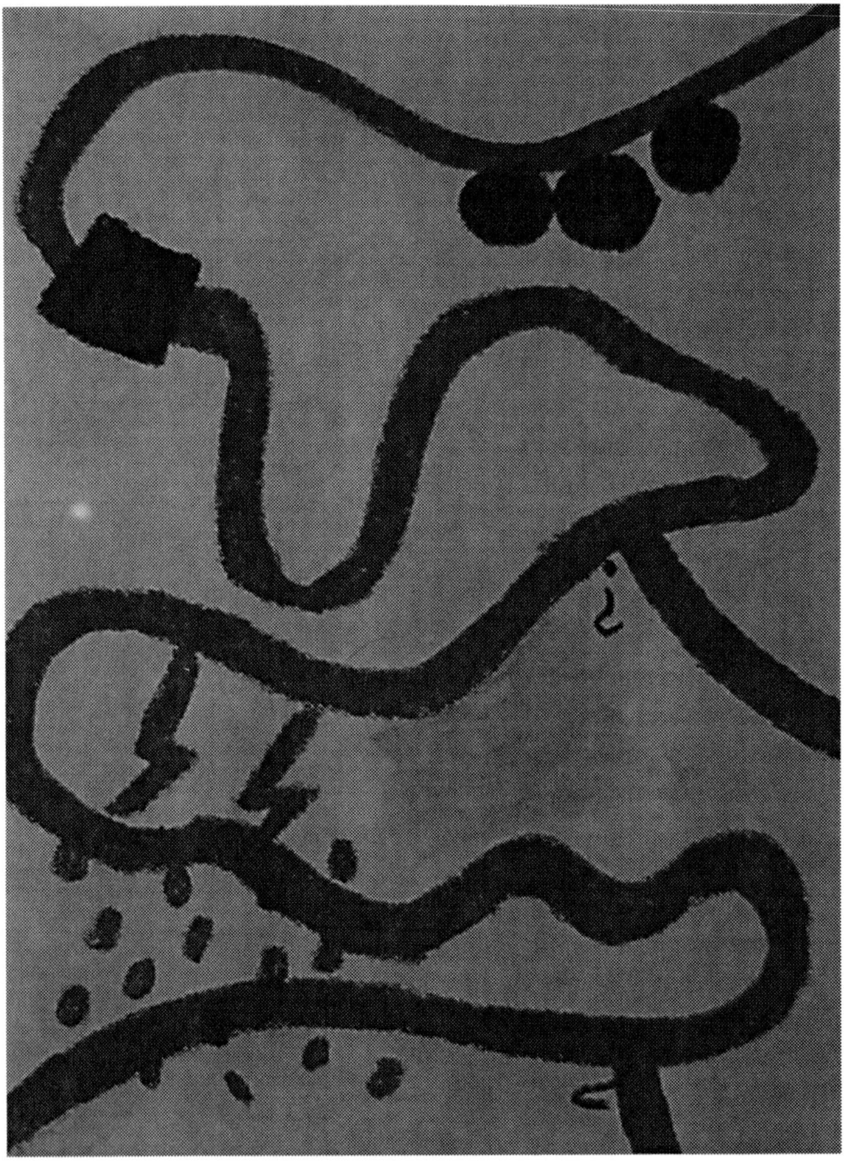

My first night away from Renfrew was difficult. I'd be staying at a hotel not far from Renfrew for the remainder of the time. I felt lonely and out of place. I was worried that I would no longer feel like part of Renfrew's community as I would be spending less time there. But I didn't feel ready yet to return home to Chicago. My memories of being there were filled with triggers.

During my first full day as a day patient, I woke up feeling very depressed. I was overwhelmed and triggered about going home. I felt safer in Renfrew's bubble than I did out in the real world. I hadn't felt this magnitude of depression since the beginning of my stay at Renfrew. I was very afraid of disconnecting from Renfrew's safe haven.

* * *

During one of my movement groups, I finally connected with my spirituality. We walked around the grounds at Renfrew and each found our own peaceful spot. In doing this, I came upon a place where I found some peace and felt a power inside that was larger than my eating disorder. The scene consisted of beautiful tall, brown grass with trees decorated with multicolored leaves and small white butterflies skimming the top of the grass, weaving themselves in and out of the reeds. I knew only God could create such a scene.

* * *

To start preparing for my return home, I met with the exercise coordinator, and she cleared me to go for a run. Even though running was still triggering for me, it was an activity that I wanted to try to return to in some capacity. She thought it would be better to try it again in this safe environment before returning to it at home. This way, I could process my thoughts and feelings about it.

So, the next weekend, I planned to go for a three-mile run. There was a beautiful scenic trail close to my hotel that I planned to use. I journaled just before I began the run. I was anxious to see if my mind-body connection had improved. I really wanted to concentrate on enjoying the run—something I hadn't been able to do in quite some time. I didn't want to or plan on using it symptomatically, but, if I'm honest, the thought of burning extra calories was very appealing.

It turned out to be a positive experience. I didn't run symptomatically. I stuck to my plan and was satisfied with my effort. It felt good to let my legs carry me. I tried to focus on the beautiful trees and water that surrounded me. This run was as close to a spiritual experience as any I'd had in quite some time. I noticed sensations, smells, and sights, but not without really concentrating. This didn't come easily. Surprisingly, I didn't miss running as much as I thought I might. That scared me, though, as I paralleled that with thinking that maybe I wouldn't miss my eating disorder as much as I thought I might. I wasn't yet ready to give it up.

* * *

One afternoon, a friend of mine and I went for a walk on this same path on which I had run. It was beautiful outside, and we wanted to enjoy the weather and have some time together to just talk. The path was packed that day with people who were out enjoying the weather just as we were. We happened to pass face-to-face with an employee at Renfrew who was out for a walk herself. She recognized us, and we recognized her as she had sat in on many of our recent groups. We all said hello and passed on our ways.

A couple of days later, word got back to my friend and me that we had "been observed running nearby Renfrew" by one of the employees. When I was made aware of this, anger filled me immediately. I didn't know how to respond. I wanted to lash out at her and question why she made up such a lie. But I knew that would be inappropriate. I felt violated and abused. How could she say such a blatant lie? And why didn't she confront my friend and me herself? I was very confused and frustrated. I feared my treatment team would take her word and not mine—that they would have to take her word. I had worked so hard at dealing with my exercise issues, and I promised myself that I would not go against Renfrew's rules regarding this. This is one reason why I was so offended at the employee's lie. I had also worked very hard at developing a trust between me and my treatment team. I didn't want that trust broken as I prepared to leave.

I discussed the situation with different members of my team, and to my surprise, they believed me that I hadn't run without permission.

I felt trusted, but my anger at the employee was only increasing. I had to confront her in some way.

So, I decided to write her a letter explaining my anger and my offended feelings. I believed in my heart that she had lied, and I needed her to know that I knew this and that she couldn't lie against me without my confronting her. My letter was direct and straight to-the-point. I told her exactly how her lie made me feel. The letter was put into her mailbox the day before I left Renfrew, and I never heard from her again. I am at peace with the situation now because I knew I had not acted on my symptoms.

I took a healthy step in reacting to this situation. I had a choice to make—cower and be stepped on or use my voice. I'm proud of myself for using my voice, small as it may have been. I recognized and expressed my anger in a healthy way.

That week had been a pivotal one for me as I'd transitioned successfully to the day program. I had also begun to pick my own foods, as well as portions at mealtime and was becoming more comfortable with that process. I had a successful therapy session with Matt and became closer with certain members in the community. My run had also been successful.

Chapter Thirteen

"My Friend"

I've loved you.
Most of the time I still do.
You've been my friend—
My solace.

You've protected me,
Yet hurt me.
You've paid attention to me,
Yet ignored me.

You've lied to me,
Making my eyes see things that supposedly aren't really there.
You've deceived me
And made me believe I'm someone I'm not.

You've kept me from myself and others.
Why do I still want you in my life
When you've hurt me so much?
I'm angry at you!

10/11/03

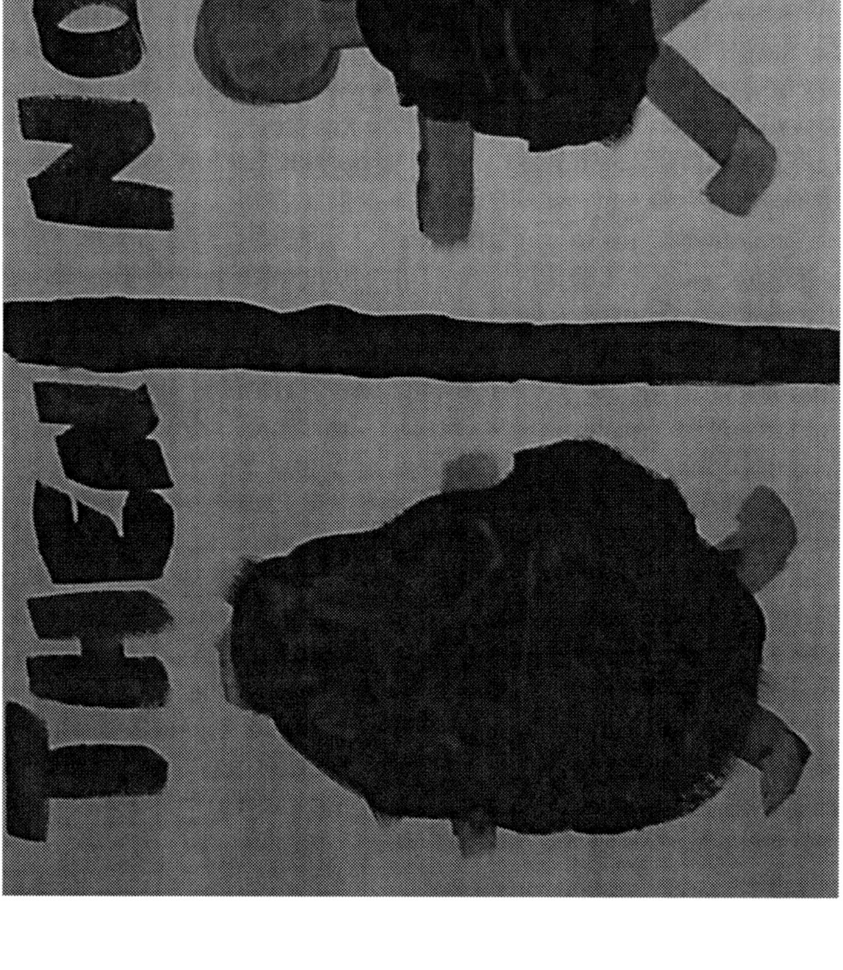
THEN
NOW

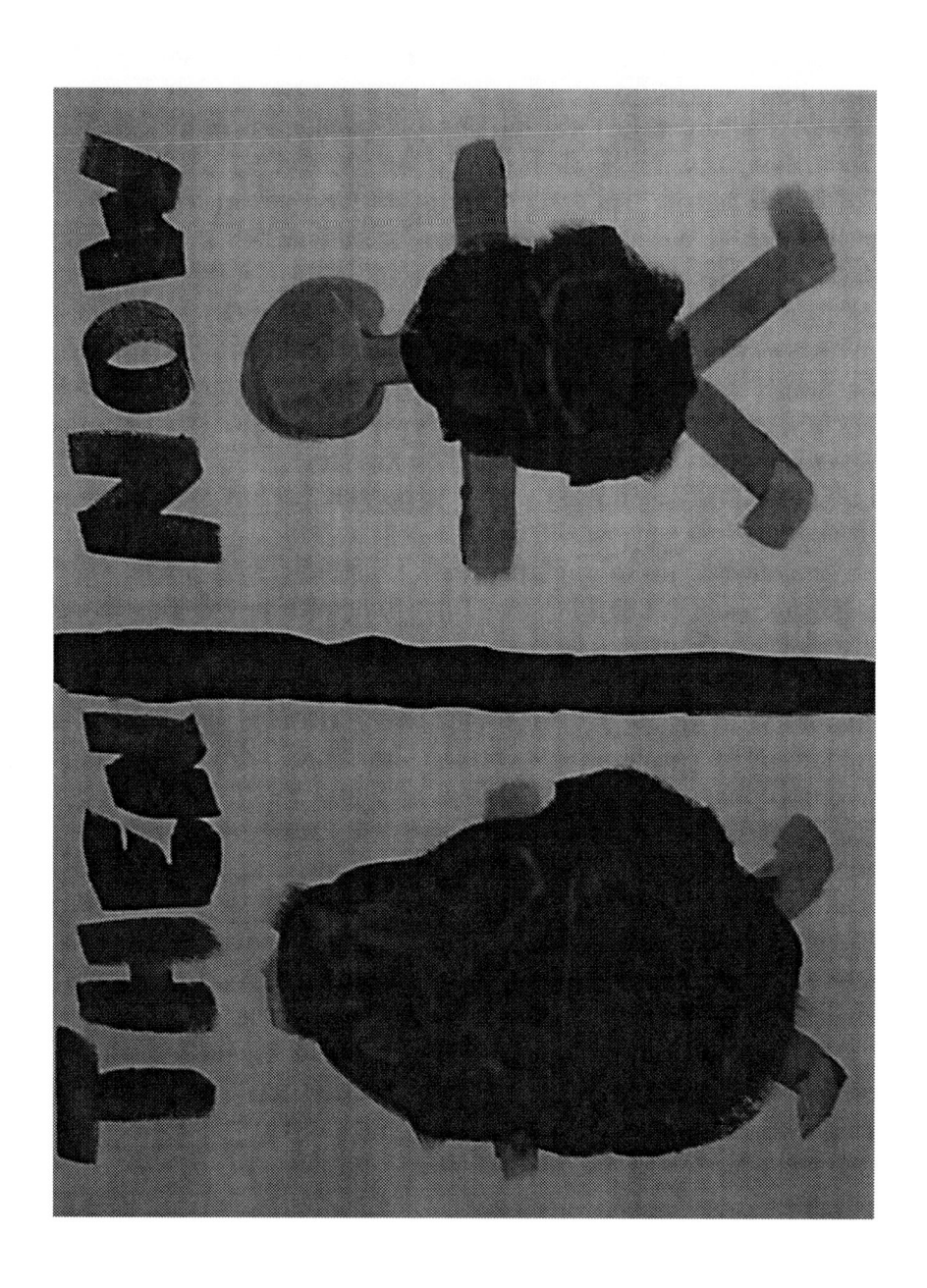

The Sunday before I left Renfrew felt like a pivotal day. Recovering from an eating disorder herself, Jessica Weiner, author of <u>A Very Hungry Girl</u>, came to speak to us all that afternoon. Her message was very powerful, and I was overcome by her words and passion. She was honest, true, and real. It was amazing to see that in a person recovering from an eating disorder. I asked her if she ever really had a time when she said to herself, "I'm done with this eating disorder. I don't need it anymore. I don't want it anymore." She said that she made the decision to not completely need it or want it the day she decided to get help for her struggles. She said she still has times when she has thoughts, desires, and urges to use her negative coping mechanisms. For her, it was all about perspective. It's how she's able to have the negative urges and thoughts but also slowly and gradually evolve them into more positive options. She told me that, even if she doesn't leave her house to take action on the positive options, her mind at least went through the thought process.

It all caused me to think that day. I figured that, in a way, I had begun to make the decision that I don't completely want this eating disorder to rule me because I, too, have sought help. I was scared, though, because I still felt like I needed it. I had doubts that I would continue with my progress when I got out of Renfrew. Would I eat? I couldn't answer that question at that point. But I knew that, when I might fall, I could always get back up.

Two of my counselors sat with me while I truly cried for the first time since my first day at Renfrew. I desperately needed to do that. And I needed to do it in front of other people, as I was doing. Jessica barely finished speaking before I lost it. The hug my counselor gave me felt so awesome. I needed someone there with me. I was so frightened about leaving Renfrew and about what lay ahead of me.

I felt completely true and real that day. I felt. I actually felt. In a way, it was refreshing. I liked how I was that day. It felt comfortable in an odd sort of way. I didn't feel fake. I think I just felt like I felt, and that was where I was, and that was okay.

* * *

A couple of days before I left Renfrew I found out my weight for a second time. I was extremely frustrated and dissatisfied by the number and the weight I had gained in the last few weeks. I tried to rationalize

I Am Enough

it. I wanted to weigh less. I still wanted to have control over it. I talked about my frustrations in one of my groups, and one of the girls told me that it didn't matter what I weighed because I would still be the same Jen. I wished I could have whole-heartedly believed that.

I'd been getting some really positive and encouraging feedback from people in my last couple of days at Renfrew. It felt so satisfying, although it also felt so uncomfortable and foreign to let some of that in. I felt undeserving of it. I was told that I'd really touched a lot of people there, and it was hard for me to let myself believe that. I felt like they'd all touched me more. People gave so much of themselves to me there. It was just unbelievable. I was so sad to leave that safe haven. I was protected there, but I needed to learn how to protect myself when I was outside of Renfrew. That really scared me. To do that, I needed to stay engaged with myself.

During my last day at Renfrew, I received a couple of wonderful pieces of advice. The first came from my therapist who told me that the work ahead would provide an opportunity for me to take a journey to really get to know myself versus being overwhelmed at all lying ahead. The second came from one of the counselors. She told me that I'd be going home to people who have known me with a certain identity, and I would now have to teach them about my new identity.

I felt stronger inside, more genuine, and more real. And I felt like I was leaving Renfrew with a better perspective on things and my recovery. <u>But</u>, I was very scared.

Chapter Fourteen

"Shame"

Shame, guilt,
Embarrassment, and strife
Have plagued me now
For most of my life.

I can't forget.
I can't forgive
Myself enough
To freely live.

Secrets have
A hold so tight.
They form a shield—
A mask so bright.

Authenticity—
It fades away—
Replaced by facades
And happiness I portray.

God's grace is free—
No truer gift.
Accepting it can heal
My internal rift.

He's with me now.
He's holding my hand.
He'll lift me up
When I cannot stand.

10/24/03

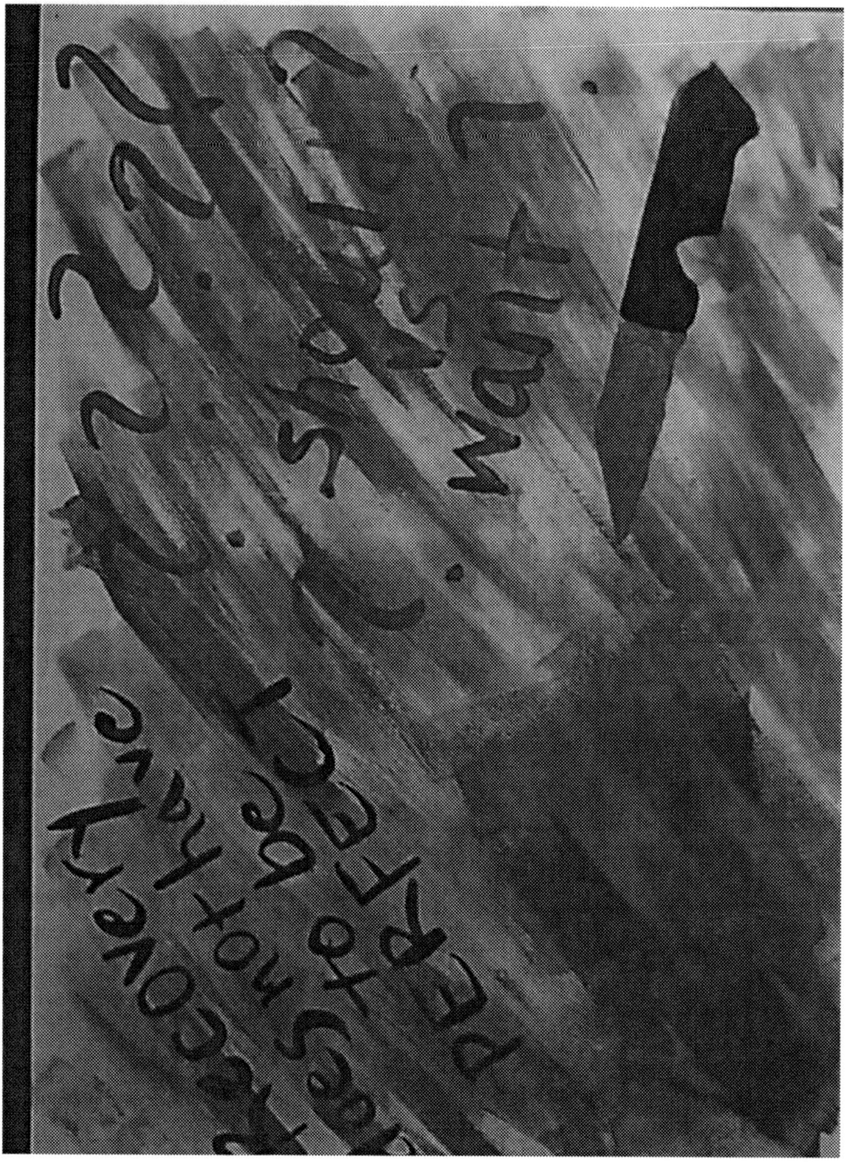

My worries about returning home were numerous. They included such things as getting in touch with friends again, returning to work, feeling overwhelmed by triggers at home, experiencing my urges to restrict, implementing a new exercise routine, socializing, communicating with Matt, getting stressed with housework, getting a therapy schedule worked out, and going home with a new identity and having the courage to convey it to others.

I needed to remember to breathe when I got home—a lot. I needed to remember that I didn't have to accomplish all those things at once and that I didn't have to be perfect. I needed to just try to be myself—whoever that is—in each moment.

* * *

We made the long drive back to Chicago from Philadelphia. It was wonderful to have the time with Matt again. It gave us a real chance to catch up on all that had happened while I was away. We stopped off in Detroit before heading the rest of the way home to visit my sister and brother-in-law. I was thankful for even the small amount of time I had to visit with my sister. I missed her greatly.

I left Renfrew immediately wanting to restrict. I knew this would be a battle ahead for me. If I was going to stick to my meal plan, I was going to need to plan out my meals very diligently. I still didn't want to eat for myself, so I was concerned about the source of my motivation to stay healthy.

When we got home, it just didn't feel good to be there. Triggers were everywhere. I didn't know how to relax in my own home. I felt out of place and very much like a stranger. Could I feel safe here again?

* * *

During my time at Renfrew, I became very concerned and confused about what to do with my work situation. So, I took two more weeks of leave to allow myself to adjust back to life in the real world. During that two weeks, I worked hard at re-adjusting. I spent long hours at coffee shops journaling, reading, writing, painting, and using the tools I had learned about at Renfrew. I was motivated. I tried my best to stay on track. I returned to seeing both my therapist and nutritionist twice a week. I also began seeing a psychiatrist to help regulate my medications. I was lucky enough to find an art therapist close to our house. I began to see her twice a month since art therapy helped me so much at Renfrew.

After that two weeks ended, I returned to work part-time. That decision was very difficult to reach. I felt guilty for not returning full-time, but I recognized that I had to build in more personal time for myself. I felt like I was staying afloat because of the time I took to journal, paint, and use my tools. I couldn't do without that now. It was difficult for me to allow myself that personal time, but I had learned it was important. Part-time work seemed the most reasonable and healthy option among the ones my boss offered to me. I knew I shouldn't return to working late evenings like I had before because I simply needed to be home for dinner.

***

I successfully implemented a new exercise regimen. I bought equipment to use at home that would help me simulate the exercise sessions at Renfrew. My running was under control, and I tried to exercise with Matt so that I didn't overdo.

I was diligent with my meal plan for the first four to six weeks I was home. I would plan and write out my meals and make sure I was getting what I needed. That lasted for a while, but, unfortunately, I slowly began restricting again. I didn't restrict to the lengths I had before I entered Renfrew, but I wanted to be thinner again. The eating disordered thoughts that had quieted became slightly louder once again. I started to feel the strength I'd gained at Renfrew begin to slip away.

***

People with eating disorders will often struggle with self-injurious behaviors. Self-injury is yet another way to punish oneself. Not long after I returned home from Renfrew, I experimented on a very minor level with self-injury. I suddenly became drawn to cutting one night. I couldn't sleep, and the idea of hurting myself felt very appealing. Matt was sound asleep, so I knew I could be alone. I went into the kitchen and took out one of our knives. I pulled my sleeve up and ran the knife lightly over my wrist. I didn't like the way it felt, so I moved higher up onto my arm. I began to scrape the inside of my arm with fairly good force with the knife. I scraped and scraped until red marks appeared and my skin began to puff up. I wanted to draw blood, so I kept scraping until it appeared. The scraping felt good. I wanted to feel the pain. I scraped until it no longer felt good. To a certain extent, I was proud of what I had done.

I waited until the next morning to tell and show Matt what I had done. He was not pleased. It scared him but for some reason did not frighten me. I had no intention to kill myself and knew very well that I was in control of whether or not I continued the behaviors. I told my therapist what I had done. We talked about it and decided that if it continued, we would need to seriously address it as a problem. It was an isolated incident that I now realize was my way of crying out that I did not want to go about my recovery trying to do it perfectly. I wanted to make mistakes. I needed to be able to let myself make mistakes and be okay with them. I needed others to let me make mistakes. Recovery does not have to be perfect. There will be slips. The important part of recovery is how we handle the slips.

* * *

I wasn't enjoying work. I loved being a physical therapist, but I wasn't enjoying my environment. It became difficult to make myself go to work. I felt self-conscious and didn't know who of my co-workers knew what about my situation. I just became more and more uncomfortable. I also knew that I didn't have much of a future with this job because, if I wanted to return to full-time work, the schedule in place at that workplace was not one to which I wanted to return. I needed a fresh start—a new environment.

I had been keeping my eyes open on the job front for some time, so I had an idea of what type of openings were out there. I knew I did not want full-time work at this point. I had a friend who worked registry at a nearby hospital, so I began to consider that as an option. Registry work is filling in for people who are sick or on vacation. The more I thought about it, the better the option seemed. It offered me more flexibility than the current job I had, and there were no stigmas. No one would have to know about my health situation. So, I updated my resume and applied for a registry position at the same hospital at which my friend worked. To my surprise, I received a job offer, which I gladly accepted. Here was my fresh start.

*　*　*

Thanksgiving rolled around several weeks after I returned home. It was at this time that I began to feel the depression part of the disease really kick itself up. I began feeling more and more down as time passed by. Matt and I went home to Kansas City for the holiday, and I had a difficult time wanting to be around others. I wanted to isolate. It's hard to enjoy a holiday with friends and family when you feel like retreating into yourself. Matt and I were at odds during the trip, so that didn't help the situation.

The next month was a downward spiral into deeper depression. I lost my motivation for working on my recovery. It took great effort to accomplish small tasks. I was restricting. I was isolating. I was nervous about starting my new job. My confidence was very low. My creativity disappeared, both on my own and in my art therapy sessions. My drive for life diminished. Spiritually, I felt very flat and like God was far away. I didn't know how to get over this hump facing me.

Christmas came and went without my feeling any of the butterflies of excitement that the holidays create. Matt and I went home again to be with our families. I didn't feel very present. Instead, I was in my head.

Chapter Fifteen

"The Fog"

How do I find my way out of this maze?
The fog just envelops me like a cloudy haze.

My mind—it races with thoughts running fast.
For some strange reason I'd like these feelings to last.

The fog is a safe place. I avoid all things there.
Numbness comes over me. I don't have to care.

No people. No stress. The world is on hold.
I keep to myself. No need to be bold.

Numbness is comfort. There's no need to feel.
The fog keeps me now from wanting to heal.

11/18/03

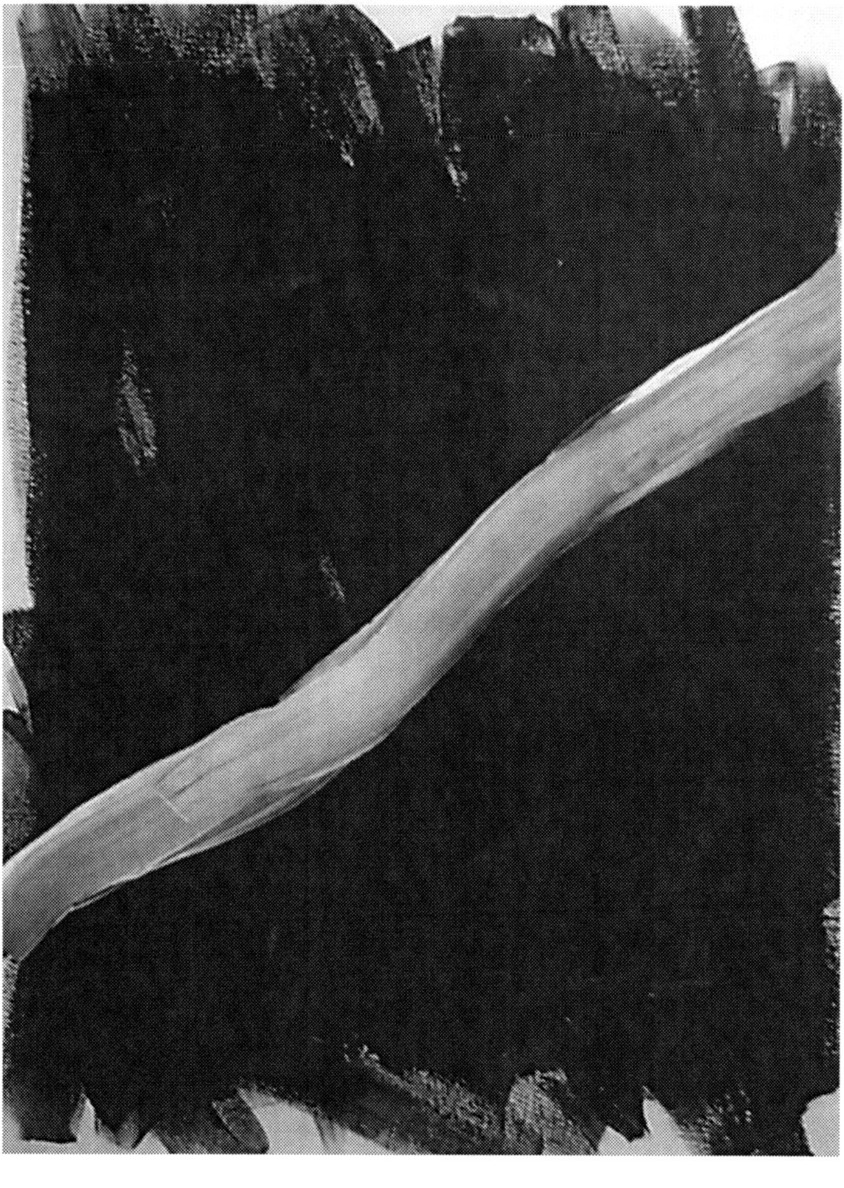

The New Year started with me anxiously awaiting my psychiatric visit a week later. I was hoping for a medication change since I was feeling worse as I took the current one. And my wish came true. My psychiatrist prescribed a different medication that would supposedly help to decrease my unmotivated feelings. I had been skeptical of medication throughout my course of therapy, so I wasn't holding my breath that it would make much of a difference.

Surprisingly, I started to feel more upbeat a couple of weeks into taking the medication. I didn't know if the medication was actually working or if I was just starting to feel better. I continue to notice a slight shift in my thinking—a shift toward the healthier side. I can't explain why. I really wish I knew the answer. It feels very surreal and unfamiliar, and somewhat dramatic. I believe that by re-feeding my body, my brain is functioning at a higher level again. Thus, I'm able to think and process in a more positive way. I've found myself questioning why I'm punishing myself as I am and as I have been. I've also started having thoughts such as, "I don't want to hurt myself anymore." I'm feeling my strength return. The course of an eating disorder is similar to that of a mountain range. There are high points and low points. This is my highest point so far, and I have hopes that I will travel even higher.

***

As my thinking becomes healthier and more positive, the eating disorder's power becomes weaker. However, the pull toward the eating disorder still exists. It still talks to me and tells me that I need it to cope. It's very easy, and somewhat appealing, to still listen to it. The eating disorder is what I've known for quite some time now. The process of letting it go is similar to the grieving process when a loved one dies. It's been a part of me for so long that it's hard to see myself without it. By trying to ignore the eating disorder now, I'm leaving behind my sense of control, my ways of coping, and my comfort zone. It's frightening to think about standing on my own two feet.

I've recently become familiar with an approach that uses the metaphor of a stoplight. Green signifies being in recovery. Yellow represents being in a slip. And red signifies being in relapse. I've found it very scary to admit that I'm in the green. I've been afraid that, if

I admit that green is where I am, people will think that my battle is suddenly over, that I'm suddenly "cured." I've also feared that to admit I'm in the green means that I'm one hundred percent ready to be free of my eating disorder. I'm not there yet.

It takes effort to be in the red zone, but I've found that it takes even more effort to be in the green. It requires consistent, positive self-reinforcement. I have to remind myself that I do not have to be in one zone completely separate from another. I need to view the lines between the zones as being blurred. I need to find the gray area and not be simply black and white in my thinking. When I think in a black and white fashion, I find myself getting stuck in an unhealthy thought pattern. I prefer to even think that there are many, many beautiful and fascinating colors between black and white—not just gray.

Chapter Sixteen

"Stoplight"

Red is relapse.
Yellow is slip.
Green is recovery.
Which way will I tip?

Red is appealing.
It's so much of what I know.
It allows me to stay sick.
I can be all alone.

Yellow is safe.
I can move somewhat forward but still hold on
To my eating disorder.
It's not yet gone.

Green is scary.
It means letting go
Of all the behaviors
And comforts I know.

To move on in life
And make it what I want
I must be authentic,
Not put on a front.

Green is where true progress
Is made and seen.
Green is where freedom
Leads me forward from where I've been.

2/26/04

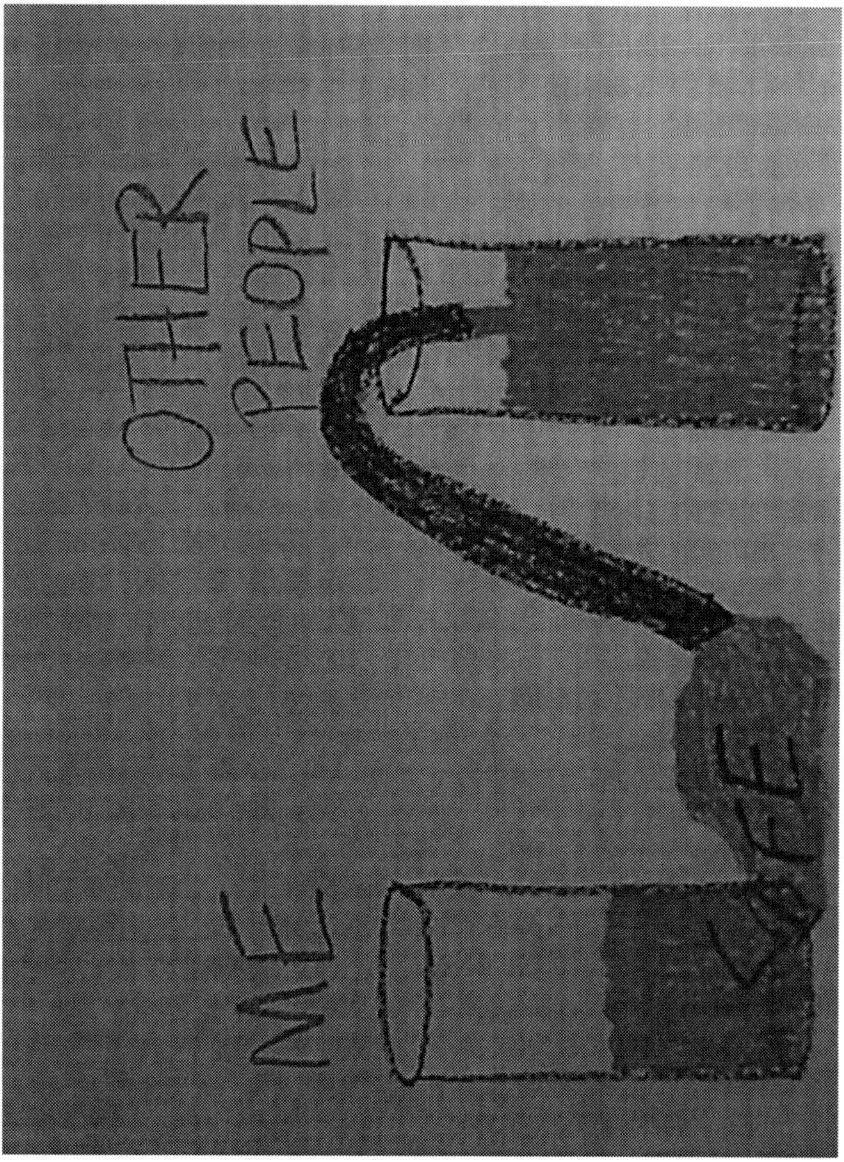
OTHER PEOPLE
ME

What does recovery mean? Each of us must define that for ourselves. To me, recovery in a rational sense means that my thoughts and actions have shifted toward a healthier lifestyle. It doesn't mean I'm striving for perfection because that would not be authentic. To be in recovery means to be authentic—true in the moment. It means beginning to believe that I am enough just as I am, without my eating disorder. It is recognizing the lies that I believe about myself and taking steps to change them into believable truths. Recovery does not mean keeping a meal plan perfectly. It does not mean that I no longer struggle. It is recognizing that I can make healthy or unhealthy choices and being able to answer the question, "What is the next best thing I can do for myself in this moment?"

I believe that one of the most difficult things to do in recovery is to put ourselves first. A person struggling with an eating disorder typically will put every person or thing he or she can find in front of him or herself. I have done this consistently throughout my life, even before my eating disorder revealed itself. As a teenager, I obsessed about pleasing my parents. Subconsciously, it was more important to me that they be happy than it was for me to be happy. When Matt struggled with depression, I would have sacrificed almost anything, including myself, to make him feel happy and content again. A hard lesson I had to learn was that I could not control other people's emotions, no matter how hard I tried, unless they allowed me to. No matter how many awards I won, I couldn't make my mom love herself. And no matter how many times I told Matt how wonderful he was, only he could help himself truly believe it.

When the eating disorder took a firm hold, I put restriction ahead of myself. I focused on denial of myself. I didn't believe that I was worthy enough to care about myself. Restriction became a way of self-punishment. My feelings of self-worth had vanished. I chose to place myself at the bottom of the barrel. I simply did not feel adequate as a person, and I felt that I should punish myself because of that. My life felt out-of-control, and it seemed like the only way to deal with that was to punish myself with restriction. So, I decided to deprive myself of a basic life necessity—food. When I couldn't control other aspects of my life, I could control what I did and did not eat.

* * *

My father was out of work for a time during my battle with anorexia. I remember having feelings that I was somehow responsible for finding him a new job. Even though he lived in Kansas City and I in Chicago, I would comb the job listings in the <u>Chicago Tribune</u> to see if I could find openings suitable for him. I didn't know what else to do. I had such overwhelming feelings of sadness and frustration for the hardship my mom and dad were enduring. I wanted to take care of them. I wanted to fix their problem.

Slowly I came to realize that the best thing I could do for them was to pray. I finally turned the situation over to God as I believed He was in ultimate control. I worked hard in therapy to come to learn and believe that my parents are adults, who can take care of themselves. It's not my responsibility as their child to protect them.

I have slowly come to learn that putting myself first is critical to my recovery. I left my full-time managerial job as a physical therapist to pursue more part-time work as a way to give myself personal time. I had to recognize that I needed a respite from the stress of the working world. I still deal with guilt that I'm not upholding my part of the bargain financially for my husband and me, but Matt has helped me come to see and understand that my health must come before my earning potential.

*　*　*

During the process of breathing, there is a very slight pause between the time when one breath is let out entirely and the next breath is drawn in. The same slight pause exists in any situation during which a decision must be made to take one path or another. It's a very small point in time during which all business stops and peace is felt. It's a time of contemplation where quietness exists. In my pause, God enters. He speaks to me and shows me what He wants me to see in that situation. My real work is done in the pause. It's the time when I stop and ask myself, "What is the next best thing that I can do for myself in this situation?" If I can keep myself in the pause, then I will move toward recovery. If I ignore the pause, I allow the world to affect my decision.

At times, I feel as though my life has no direction. My mind seems scattered, and it's hard to visualize where I'm going with my recovery.

During these times, my type-A personality often pushes me to feel as though I need to push harder and do more to further my recovery. Oftentimes, I feel like I need to figure it all out. I have found, though, that many times I need to do just the opposite. During these times of no direction, I need to simply sit with myself. I say simply, knowing that sitting with myself is often easier said than done. In essence, I need to let myself be right where I am "in the pause." If my direction seems clouded, then so be it. Trying to push through these times will often make me more confused. I'm learning to take deep breaths, relax, and enjoy the moment in which I am. When I'm able to let myself be where I am, the direction gradually begins to return.

Chapter Seventeen

"When Is It Time?"

When is it time
To give up this lie?
How can I be sure
That without it I'll survive?

It scares me to think
Of living life alone
Without my eating disorder
Leading me home.

Most of me wants
To hold on so tight.
But a small part of me still dreams
Of following the healing light.

How do I find
The strength to let go
Of something so terrible
That has befriended me so?

9/14/03

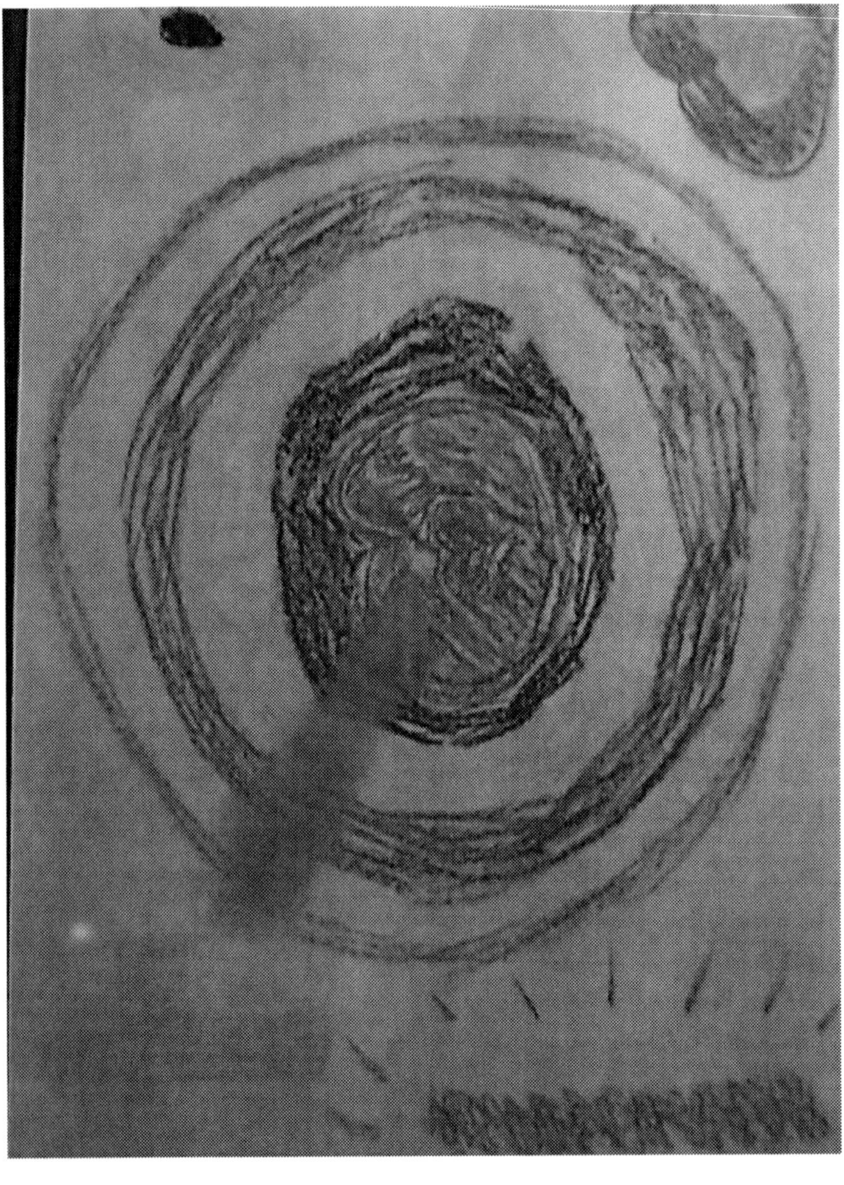

I believe very strongly in the importance of counseling during recovery from an eating disorder. For myself, it is a necessity. I have been blessed with an amazing Christian counselor who has helped me process innumerable issues. My father once said that he believes every person could benefit from therapy. I agree. Processing thoughts, feelings, and emotions with someone who has an outside professional view is an amazing experience. My therapist has led me to discover aspects of my inner self that I never knew existed. I've gained perspective on who I am as a person and on how my past has affected me. When I haven't been able to trust others, I have been able to confide in her and seek guidance from her. In therapy, I feel safe to reveal my inner thoughts and fears and explore scary issues that I wouldn't tackle on my own.

One of the most important things I've learned through therapy is how to recognize my own feelings and emotions. It's been harder for me to do this than it would seem. In the past, if I felt anger, I would stuff it down so deeply that I wouldn't even be able to realize that anger was exactly what I was feeling. The next step I took was to learn how to verbalize and express my feelings and emotions in an appropriate way once I recognized them. Essentially, this means that I discovered and learned that I had a voice which could be used to meet my needs.

Also in therapy I've developed a vision for my future. Envisioning what I would like my life to be like without my eating disorder has been one of my main motivations to work toward in recovery. Therapy has given me tools that help me to stay focused on recovery. Seeing my therapist regularly has kept me accountable to do the personal work demanded by recovery from an eating disorder.

In addition to outpatient therapy, it has been imperative that I see a nutritionist regularly. Basically, I needed someone to teach me how to eat again. Nutrition therapy is a very practical approach to a basic and necessary behavior—eating. It deals with the here and now—what I will eat for my next meal. My nutritionist has helped me develop a personalized meal plan. She has taught me how to structure my day to gain the proper energy requirements as well as how to correlate my food needs with exercising.

My nutritionist has helped me face one of my most feared issues—weight and how to deal with weight changes. She encourages me to meet the goals we set. She is extremely patient with me, especially when I tell her I will perform a certain behavior and leave her office knowing I am not going to do it. I have learned to trust my nutritionist immensely. I've had fears that I would take eating to another extreme and gain tremendous amounts of weight once I started eating properly again. She has calmed my fears and has helped me reach a healthy weight without going overboard.

Through my eating disorder, I have discovered my creative aspects for expression. Art therapy has become a creative outlet for me, allowing me to express my thoughts, feelings and emotions. I royally surprised myself in my art therapy groups at Renfrew, finding a tool that I could use on my own. Through art I was able to really access feelings that I hadn't been able to access before on my own. My art gives me visions to connect with my feelings. My artwork provides a visual diary of my path through my eating disorder as art gives me concrete pictures to return to, reminding me of different phases of my recovery.

We often speak of tools in recovery. Art became one tool to use when dealing with thoughts and feelings, instead of using my symptoms. I have other tools as well. I began to write poems. I had never done this before, but in the midst of my eating disorder, the words seemed to come to me, especially words of anger and sadness. Journaling is another tool that I've been able to use quite effectively.

My journal is my own special place to explore my thoughts and feelings. It's safe. The content is known only to me, unless I allow others to read it. As I write, I often realize perspectives, feelings, and thoughts that I had not experienced before. Any emotion I feel can be expressed through words. I will often use my journal to write letters that I never send to different people. My therapist always tells me that I'm never at a loss for something to write about. She says that even if my mind seems empty or blank, then I can write about the emptiness. It's often in the emptiness that some of my deepest feelings are found.

* * *

Eating disorders can be viewed as family diseases. Of course, one person is directly affected by struggling with the actual disease, but other family members, even those not living in the same household with the identified patient, are indirectly affected. This means that each person has a responsibility to deal with his or her part of the issue.

Family members and friends often say they just want to be able to do something to help. I believe that the single most important thing family members or friends can do to help a person struggling with an eating disorder is to make themselves and their relationship with the identified patient as healthy as possible. In many cases, this may mean that the support person should enter his or her own counseling. By building healthy relationships with others, the struggling patient will feel more able to take care of him or herself and not stay stuck in a cycle of dependency.

My husband has given me a gift as he has done his own counseling regarding my eating disorder. He has worked hard on his own issues to make himself as strong and healthy as possible so that he is able to interact properly with me. In addition, we have done quite a bit of couple's counseling. This has been important work for us to do, especially with the illness occurring early in our marriage. We have been in couple's counseling since months prior to our wedding. We began it when Matt was struggling so much with his issues and have continued it throughout my struggles. We've explored issues including communication, intimacy, family, money, and many more. We were blessed earlier in our relationship to have a Christian counselor who led us spiritually as well. We've learned so much about each other and our relationship by remaining in couple's counseling.

* * *

Family therapy has been another important part of my recovery process. This has included sessions with Matt, myself, and my parents as well as individual sessions with just myself and my parents. Thankfully, my parents have realized that participation in therapy is the most important way to help me. Much of my therapy has centered around family issues as well as my childhood. Earlier in my recovery process, I came across some frustrations from my childhood that my therapist and I felt should be discussed with my parents. I needed to tell them that I was angry at the way dynamics played out in our family. My mom didn't think her restricting patterns were affecting our family, and my dad basically ignored it. I grew up feeling that I needed to take care of my mother —that she was fragile. I was terrified of hurting my parents by saying these things. I wanted to protect them, but the only way to grow was to take the risk and trust that my parents could handle the things I had to say to them.

A face-to-face discussion was too scary to think about, so I wrote everything in a letter and sent it to them. They processed the letter with their own therapist, and then we met in Chicago for a family therapy session with my therapist. It was a difficult session but a powerful one. They each wrote their own response letter to me expressing their love and concern. Matt was a part of the session as well. It was much easier to face my parents knowing that my therapist was there to facilitate the session. It was a positive experience.

My parents flew to Philadelphia when I was at Renfrew to participate in another family session with me. It was equally as powerful. Addressing more of my anger, I wrote another letter that I read to them in the session. Love between all of us was definitely expressed, and we came away from the session having a better understanding of our relationship.

My parents love me enough that they agreed to do their own couple's counseling in Kansas City. This gave them an opportunity to address their own fears and frustrations about my eating disorder as well as their own personal issues. I love them so much for the work they've done to make themselves and our relationship as healthy as possible.

My sister was eager to do whatever she could to help as well. So, I bought her a journal and asked her to journal as much as she wanted about our family, our childhood, her relationship with my parents, her relationship with me, how she views my eating disorder, and what she feels is her role in the process. She was so willing for me to read what she wrote, and it gave me insights that I'd never known before. Karyn has always been at the top of my support list. She used to be the "grown up" and sit with me when I would shake from fear in my bed at night as a child. The way she has treated me and interacted with me in relation to my eating disorder has meant so much. She has trusted me. She tells me that she has faith that I can beat this disorder and can handle my struggles by standing on my own two feet. Her confidence in me has boosted my confidence in myself.

Chapter Eighteen

"Therefore I tell you, do not worry about your life, what you will eat; or what you will wear. Life is more than food!"
Luke 12:22-23

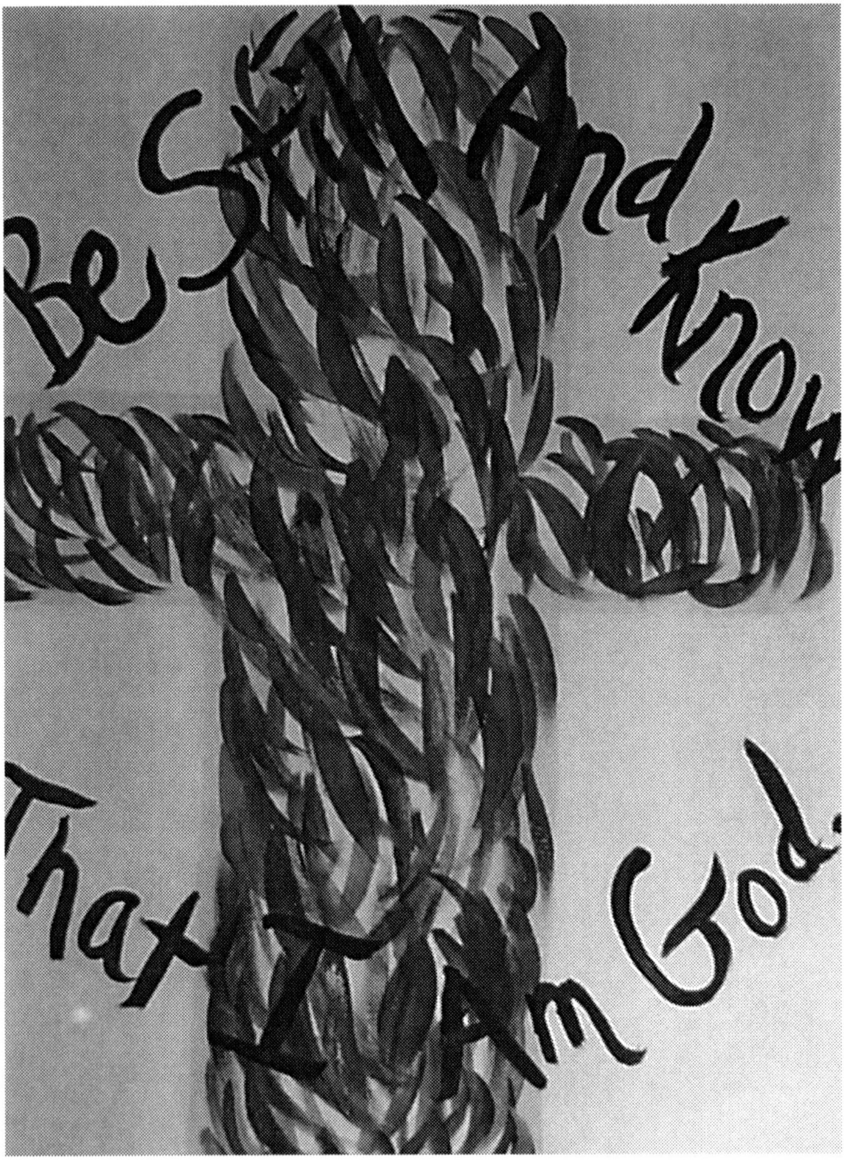
Be Still And know
That I Am God.

I Am Enough

My Christian faith has always been a very important part of my life. I've gone to church ever since I was a baby. My parents have set wonderful Christian examples. I believe wholeheartedly that God loves me and that His grace sets me free.

As a child, faith seemed so easy. The older *I've* become, the more confusing *it's* become. I grew up believing what I believed because my parents told me to. I went to church because it was just what we did. It was expected. Thinking back on that part of my life, it now seems like my faith was a result of circumstance. I was born into a strong Christian family; therefore, I would be a strong Christian as well. I knew all the details of my faith. I went to all the confirmation classes. I memorized all the creeds and prayers. Now, during this time of my life, I see back then that I had faith, but it never seemed to grow into my own very personal faith with God.

I've struggled numerous times with the following question: Do I believe what I believe because it's what I grew up being told to believe, or do I believe what I believe because I have personally made that choice? I've come to the conclusion that my beliefs are a result of my own choices but only because God has led me to this place. I'm very thankful for that.

I thought I would have grown closer to God and stronger in my faith as I've traveled through this valley of my life. But instead, I have struggled with my faith. I know and believe wholeheartedly that God is with me, but He just feels *so* distant. I don't feel like I've been able to relinquish control of my life into God's hands. Instead, I've tried to keep all the control to myself. I haven't completely trusted that God will take care of me and will see me through this season of my life. *"I consider that our present sufferings are not worth comparing with the glory that will be revealed in us" (Romans 8:18).*

I have felt that I need to be constantly *doing* something to be worthy of God's love. In my heart I know that my worth is not based on my productivity. Unfortunately, I think it just makes *me* feel better to always be doing instead of just being. A verse that has spoken to me loudly over the past couple of years is, *"Be still and know that I am God" (Psalm 46:10).* It is a big challenge for me. Hearing that verse really does cause me to stop in my tracks and realize that I need to slow down and take refuge in knowing that God is in control. I do not have to be in control.

God has blessed me so incredibly by putting my Christian counselor in my life. Treatment has been approached with a Christian component. For me to be truly genuine and honest about myself, this includes discussing my faith. It has meant so much to me that I have been able to be honest with her about where I am with my faith. In turn, she has so generously shared her personal beliefs and mature faith with me. I believe that true recovery for me would not be possible if God were not in my life. I would not be able to face this eating disorder on my own. As my therapist has shown me, I am powerless over my eating disorder. But God is not. As I said earlier, even though God feels distant, I still know He is there.

My treatment sessions often include my therapist praying. It's such a powerful experience to hear someone praying for me. She has often asked God to reveal to me what He wants me to see about myself, my past, my present, or my future. It has felt so special to hear my therapist pray for me because I've struggled so much with personal prayer. For some reason, I haven't felt like I've wanted to talk to God. Maybe it's because I don't know where to start. I feel like I don't know what to say. In turn, I am afraid I don't know how to listen to God.

My therapist has said to me that even though I feel spiritually empty, I must still make myself available for God to do His work in me. I need to put myself in situations where I am reminded of God's grace. What an amazing gift! *"My grace is sufficient for you"* (II Corinthians 12:9). I think I oftentimes try to earn God's grace even though it's a gift freely given to me. No matter how hard I try to earn it, I never measure up. And when I don't measure up, I feel worthless. I have an index card that I carry around with me on which I have written the following phrase, " I am worthwhile because I am a child of God and He made me as the unique person I am." Because I am a sinner, I am not worthy of God's grace, but He still offers it to me if I believe that He died for my sins. John 7:38 is a great reminder that "whoever believes in me, as the Scripture has said, streams of living water will flow from within him."

I recently attended a Women of Faith conference and was moved by the passion for Christ that the speakers and musicians displayed.

I Am Enough

Their spirits seemed to pour out of them. As I heard them speak of their personal relationships with God, I was reminded that God desires the same kind of relationship with me. He created me and knows me intimately. He is my greatest supporter, especially during times of struggle. By opening myself and my heart to God, He will come closer and lead me every step of the way. Even if the road seems to dead end or take a direction I was not anticipating, God will lead me right where He wants me to be. One of the speakers at the conference spoke of God's will. She reminded me that God does have a plan for my life. Hard as it may be, trusting in His will is the only way.

Trusting is difficult for me. I struggle with believing that God's promises will be fulfilled in my life. Brennan Manning's book, <u>Ruthless Trust</u>, has opened my eyes to understanding trust on a deeper level. He writes of trust being the "winsome wedding of faith and hope." He states, "Faith arises from the personal experience of Jesus as Lord. Hope is reliance on the promise of Jesus, accompanied by the expectation of fulfillment." For me, faith is the easier part of the equation. Instead of relying wholeheartedly on Jesus' promise, I will often submit to my own earthly fears. I allow doubt to enter in. Manning also writes, "Trust in Jesus grows as we shift from making self-conscious efforts to be good to allowing ourselves to be loved as we are (not as we should be)." I struggle with accepting myself just as I am. God loves me simply because I'm His child. My question is—how do I increase my trust in God? Manning's answer is "I cannot simply will myself to trust. What does lie within my power is paying attention to the faithfulness of Jesus."

I do not believe that God is punishing me by allowing this time of struggle in my life. I do believe that it is part of His plan for my life that I face what I am facing. I have faith that God intends for good to come from my struggles. God is slowly revealing to me His purposes for my eating disorder. For example, I need to get to know myself better. In the past, I've struggled with the answer to the question, "Who am I?" I now feel that I am able to begin to formulate an answer. I need to learn how to take care of myself—God's creation. I need to resolve situations that occurred during my childhood. I need to learn how to recognize and express my emotions. Matt and I need to learn how to communicate more effectively. I need to make my

Jennifer D. Calvin

relationship with Mom and Dad healthier and more balanced. I need to simply find balance in my own life. And probably most importantly, I need to wrestle with my faith to begin to really make it my own. I've begun to make progress in regards to all of these purposes, and I know that God will continue to lead me to grow.

Chapter Nineteen

"My Voice"

People don't know.
They don't understand
How their words can hurt.
They can burn like a brand.

Or the lack of words
Makes me feel they don't care.
My silent scream unheard.
I'm starving to make them aware.

"Hear me!" I scream.
"I have things to say."
My silent words go unnoticed.
My unheard voices fade away.

I'm angry at people.
They don't seem to see.
I'm fighting this battle
Because I don't know the true me.

Someday I'll scream.
"Hear me!" I'll say.
"I'm just as important
As you are today."

My voice will ring loud,
Confident and true.
I won't need to starve
Myself to be true.

9/14/03

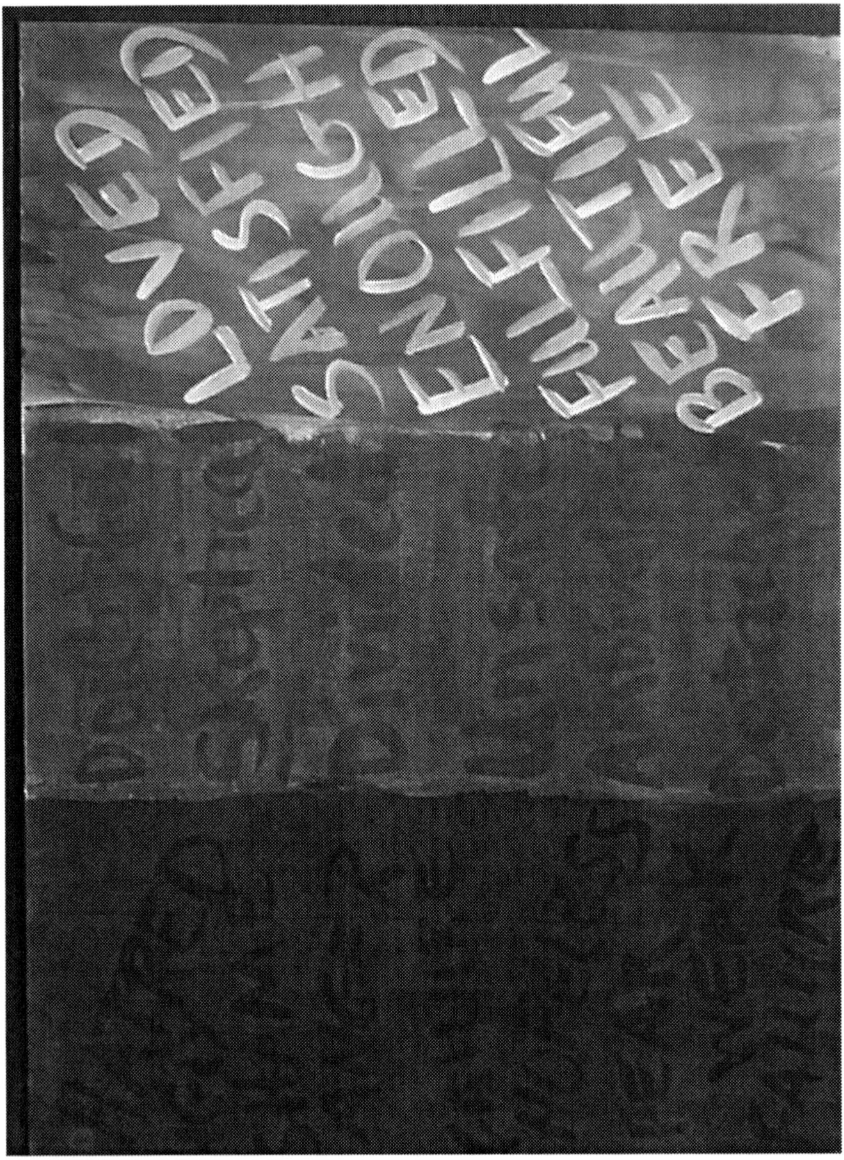

During my recovery, redefining relationships of all kinds has become important. As I travel through recovery, I am evolving as a person, and my relationships must evolve with me. I have to continually ask myself, "Is this a healthy relationship for me to be a part of?" If it is not, then I must discover the unhealthy parts and work to change them. For me, this means I must successfully convey to others what I personally need from the relationship and what I need to change. Through this process, healthy relationships can usually be maintained.

* * *

One of the most frustrating things for me is people assuming that, just because I'm beginning to feel better, my battle is over. It's certainly not that easy. And I'm not sure that I want it to be that easy. The road to recovery is my personal journey to becoming a stronger person. We often discover our true strength in the midst of our struggles. I believe that I was meant to travel this path, but it's been the most difficult trip I've ever taken. I want to share an excerpt from my journal.

> Recovery is **so** hard. Things can be moving along nicely and then WHAM! Out of the blue, I can be triggered in an instant.
>
> This afternoon was rough. I was weighed today at my nutritionist's visit. My weight has been stable over the last few weeks at a number that I've gotten myself to be okay with. I've been feeling good. But today, after not being weighed in two weeks, I found out that my weight has increased by six pounds! I felt shell-shocked. I was instantly flooded with eating disorder thoughts. I felt like a failure. I was disgusted with myself. I felt like I'd lost my willpower.
>
> I'm not sure that Kate wanted to tell me my weight today. I pressed her to. I've never really wanted to know my weight in the past for fear that I'd become obsessed with it. That's exactly what's happened over the past few weeks.
>
> Kate was so great to help me think as rationally as I could during my frustration. We made lists of pros and cons of being in the eating disorder versus being healthier. I need to remember that a number is a number and it doesn't define who I am as a person.
>
> I know the best and most healthy thing to do is to keep eating, but I want to restrict. It's so easy to revert right back to the eating disorder.

Maybe I need to go back to being blind weighed. I've trusted Kate with my weight thus far, and I know she won't lead me astray.

I'm trying to make every excuse as to why I would have gained weight. I haven't changed my food intake or my work out routine in the last couple of weeks. There's no reason that I would have gained weight, so maybe my body is still trying to find its set point. When does this become easier?

I believe that I will always have a tendency toward eating disordered behaviors and be susceptible to eating disordered thoughts to some degree. However, I will not make the choice to always act on them. I have been working hard with my therapist on developing a vision of the "healthy me." I envision myself as a mom, feeling comfortable on social outings, and just enjoying life. Envisioning these dreams has helped me believe that they really can come true. I will be healthy, balanced, and authentic. I am working hard at believing that I am enough just as I am. I will fall down. I will have slips. But my strength will allow me to pull myself back into balance. I have a magnet on my refrigerator that says "follow your bliss." And that's exactly what I intend to do.

AFTERWARDS

One hope of mine in writing this book is that it would appeal not only to those struggling personally with an eating disorder but the support people who are affected and involved as well. In addition, I wanted to give those in my circle an opportunity to share their own thoughts and perspectives, both personally and professionally. I believe this story is not solely mine. Those who have written these afterwards have all been personally affected by and involved with my eating disorder. They have and are still walking with me on this journey. I love and hold each one of them close to my heart.

My husband:

When Jen asked me to write something for this book, I started to think about what I could contribute that might be helpful to other spouses, family members, or friends who serve as support for someone with an eating disorder. I am not an expert. I am not a trained professional in dealing with eating disorders. I will not presume to offer "advice" to others. All I can offer is my own personal experience. I know, personally, I have been very thankful to other support people who have shared their stories with me and allowed me to learn from their experiences.

I have identified three keys that have been important to my experiences of supporting my wife and our marriage in her survival and ongoing recovery from an eating disorder.

1) Practice unconditional love
2) Find my own support system
3) Communicate honestly and "refuse to walk on eggshells"

Unconditional Love

When I stood at the altar with Jen a little over three years ago and said the words "I do," I took that promise very seriously. Looking back now, I had no idea what we were getting into. Our married life together has not been what we had planned or expected. We have faced many more challenges than either one of us could have dreamed of. Through all these challenges, one thing that has kept us together has been our unconditional love and commitment to one another.

Jennifer and I both feel very blessed to come from two families that exemplify strong Christian family values. As children, long before we ever met each other, we were both being taught the meaning of unconditional love and commitment to marriage. That value is at the root of who we both are as people. That value has served us well in our own marriage.

Eating disorders are very hurtful and disruptive things. I have heard of countless stories of families that have been so hurt that relationships have been permanently damaged or abandoned. From what I have seen, an eating disorder is such a powerful force on the family that it either tears the family apart or draws it closer together. We have worked very hard at making sure our experiences brought us closer together.

Eating disorders attack at the very root of a person. Jennifer has gone through tremendous changes as a person. I can honestly say she is not the same person that I married. I am sure she could say that same thing about me. We had two options: be disappointed and give up because we were changing, or learn to love the new person even more. It was not always easy, but we have made a commitment to love each other unconditionally.

Unconditional love can be as hard for the eating disordered person to receive as it can be for the support people to give. When Jen was in the depths of her disorder, she was so depressed that she felt worthless. She could not understand why I would want to stick around and love her through all that was happening. She often had trouble believing and trusting that I could love her. I think I was often able to love her when she couldn't love herself. I found little ways to demonstrate my love for her. I adopted the saying "I am not going anywhere." No matter how bad things got, I would say those words to her and reassure her of my commitment to her.

I have had friends tell me that they don't know if they could have done what I have done in staying with my wife through all we have been through. I never know how to respond to that. I believe that love is a choice—not a feeling. If you truly choose to love someone, how could you not stay with them? I am happy to say that while the experience was challenging, our love and commitment is even stronger today than the day we said "I do." Because of our unconditional love, we have been able to grow together and experience the gift that comes from a deeply committed relationship.

Finding My Own Support System

I, by nature, am a very social person. I thrive on social interactions. Eating disorders, by nature, are very anti-social diseases. The eating disorder thrives on low self-esteem, secrecy, and isolation. As Jen slipped deeper into her eating disorder, she became increasingly uncomfortable in social situations. As her isolation increased, our social life as a couple also decreased. This proved to be very difficult for me to handle. I had to find a way to respect her growing discomfort with social situations, while at the same time provide for my own social needs to avoid feeling isolated myself.

As a newly married couple, I felt that was our time to be making friends together and to be developing a social identity for us as a couple. At the same time, due to the eating disorder, Jen was slowly distancing herself from both her personal friends and our "couple friends." I initially felt like I needed to go along with her and be supportive of her needs. As the eating disorder became more severe, the level of social isolation increased, both for Jen personally and for us as a couple. It finally got to the point that Jen not only isolated from social situations but isolated from me personally as well. I was hurt. I began to feel very isolated myself, but I felt guilty asking Jen to go to social events where I knew she would be uncomfortable. I felt even more guilt to think about doing things without her. I got married so that I would have someone else to share my friends and experiences with. I didn't want to leave her behind, but I began to learn that I had to find ways to take care of myself.

I became very intentional about providing a support system for myself. This support system took many different forms. In the height of Jen's disorder, she was not able to communicate on an intimate level. Eating disorders are very private things with some social stigmas attached. During the early stages of Jen's disorder, we chose to only share what was going on with a select few. It was important to us to protect our privacy and our marriage, but this decision also added to the isolation. I began to feel as I was carrying this "big secret." I believe it is virtually impossible to carry something as devastating as an eating disorder and remain emotionally healthy without having a close support system. I needed people I could turn to, talk to, vent to, and just share everyday conversation with. I began by reaching out to family. Both Jennifer's and my family have been extremely supportive. Even though my family was out of state, I was always only a phone call away. Beyond that support of family, it was also important to have some close friends who knew what was going on. While it was initially difficult to share something that personal with others and ask for help, the risk has been well worth it. I felt very blessed to have both male and female friends, as well as family, that I could confide in and communicate with on a very personal level. I will not name names, but to those of you close friends and family who are reading this book, I thank God for you.

Beyond the intimate support from close friends, I found it equally important to establish an everyday network of friends and social activities. Because we had only lived in the Chicago area for a few years, I did not have a pre-established friend base. I became very intentional about connecting with the friends that I did have and creating new friendships wherever possible. Very simple activities such as going out for a beer after work or watching football on Sundays with a couple of friends became very "therapeutic" and important for me. I became intentional about getting involved in activities. I got involved in various church sports and activities. I reached out to some people from work and worked hard at social relationships. I got involved in social activities through my university graduate program. Establishing as many everyday relationships and activities proved to be very valuable in maintaining a certain level of normalcy in an otherwise very difficult time. Most of these people to this day still do not know the situation that Jen and I are dealing with, but their social friendships have been, nevertheless, instrumental in supporting me in the toughest times.

The final type of support system that has been important to me, and that I would like to advocate, is that of support groups and professional counseling. When we first identified Jen's eating disorder, we were already working with a couple's counselor. It was our counselor with whom Jen was first able to share her concerns about her eating disorder. She was able to give us encouragement and reassurance as a couple as well as providing referrals to get Jen help. I know Jen has already advocated for counseling in the body of the book, but I feel that it was equally important for me as a support person. There are so many fears and concerns that I as a support person needed to work through. I have found both personal and couple's counseling to be invaluable to me in both maintaining my own mental health as well as helping my wife in her recovery. Our counselors were also able to provide much needed information through educational resources and support groups.

When I first heard the word "anorexia," I had a lot of fear and very little knowledge of the disorder. I found a local chapter of an eating disorder support group. I began attending these meetings by myself. At first, Jen did not want to attend, so I went for myself. It was so helpful to hear other eating disordered patients as well as their support friends and family talk about their experiences. This support group was able to take away some of the secrecy and isolation for me. Here was a group of people going through similar experiences as my wife and I were. I wasn't alone any more! For about 6 months to a year, I was the only male to regularly attend the group by myself. Despite this fact, I felt completely accepted. When the time was right, Jen eventually reached a point in her recovery that she felt comfortable enough to begin attending the meetings with me. Having her attend the group with me made it that much better. That group has become a very special and important part of our recovery process. I have just recently had another obligation that has conflicted with our group meetings. This support system has served us both so well. Jen now continues to attend the meeting alone and give me reports. I actually look forward to the time when I, too, can return to this support system.

As Jen continues her recovery, she is becoming more comfortable again socially, both with me and with others. I am finding my need for support from others is feeling less urgent and less intense. I am once again learning to depend on her for my primary support. We are also becoming more socially active again. We are now having that opportunity to create a social identity for ourselves as a couple. Through this whole experience, I feel I have become more appreciative of the human need to interact with and feel supported by others. I am more appreciative of both my relationships with others and of my relationship with my wife.

Communicate Honestly and Refuse To "Walk on Eggshells!"

Eating disorders provide a very powerful form of communication. Even though the behaviors and the results are destructive, the disorder provides the individual with a way to communicate emotions that he or she doesn't feel otherwise able to communicate. Friends and family are left to try to interpret and make sense of behaviors that don't seem to make sense. It has been my experience that communication is the first thing to go, and the most important thing to restore, in the living with and recovery from an eating disorder.

Communication has always come naturally to me. I am a "talker" by nature, and a teacher by trade; I have always felt that I am a fairly effective communicator. While I still generally believe that, I have learned much more than I thought possible about communication. Most importantly, I have learned that talking is only half of the communication process. I have had to work very hard at learning to listen to the messages that my wife is sending me. I have learned that communication is truly a two-way street, and that her message to me is just as important as my message to her. I have also gained a respect for how much effort good communication requires and how hard we have worked to improve ours. This disorder which originally greatly interrupted our communication, has, in the end, greatly improved our communication.

I have noticed a common theme between my own experiences and the stories of others in regards to communication and eating disorders. There often seems to be a tendency to "walk on egg shells." Eating disordered people are unable to communicate their true emotions, so they hold their feelings back, and they come out through the eating disorder. Those closest to the individual become confused and hurt and are afraid to communicate honestly out of fear for making the situation worse. Others simply don't know what to say, so they say nothing at all.

In my experience, my wife became tired of always doing things because "she should" or to please others. She wanted to use her voice, to have others listen to her needs and wants, but she was afraid of the response of others. All her life, she had "walked on eggshells" and held back her true feelings. These feelings eventually expressed themselves through her eating disorder. As her husband, I was unsure of what my role was. I didn't know whether to love her and support her decisions, or whether I needed to protect her by playing "food police." Friends and family often expressed concern to me for Jen's well being, but they were at a loss for how to act around her or what to say. Everyone was unsure, and as a result, was "walking on eggshells."

Through these experiences and much trial and error, Jen and I have adopted the motto, "Refuse to walk on eggshells." We have tried it and discovered that we simply cannot live that way. The fact of the matter is there is no "right thing to say." All you can say is what you feel, and all you can do is be honest. We have found it much easier to just be honest and say whatever needs to be said and deal with the results, rather than wasting time and energy trying to do or say the "right thing." We have found honest communication to be a key to our relationship.

Now that I have identified the need for honest communication, I do not mean to imply that it is always easy. Jen and I continue to struggle with this. I am sure we will always struggle with this in some way. Good communication requires constant effort and attention. We continue to work on this daily. As our communication skills have improved, we have also discovered a need to educate others on communication. I continually have to encourage others to communicate directly with Jen and to not treat her as if she is "sick". Jen has had to educate others of her needs and feelings. She has found that some people around her have had trouble learning to accept her new style of communication. She has had to redefine many of her relationships and has even had to end a few that were unhealthy. Using good communication with each other and with others, we continue to repair damaged relationships and strengthen existing ones.

We, by no means, are completely past our struggles with this eating disorder. Jen continues to work hard on her recovery. I continue to learn more about her, myself, and her eating disorder in an effort to support her. She still struggles with food. I still struggle personally. We still struggle as a couple. I know that there is always the potential that her disorder will reoccur. I know that she will probably always struggle on some level with food. I know we will always have our own struggles. I also know that we have learned a lot from this experience. I know that we have been through a very difficult situation and have come out stronger on the other side. I have seen the same happen in the lives of others that have shared their stories with me. I know the same can happen for others that will deal with eating disorders (or any other challenge) in the future. My hope and prayer is that God will use my wife's and my experience and story to help someone else in the same way that He has used the experiences and stories of others to help me.

Matthew K. Calvin

My parents:

Our daughter, Jennifer, is facing a serious illness—anorexia. As her parents, we have moved through a wide range of emotions since learning of this diagnosis two years ago: fear, sorrow, guilt, anger, helplessness, hope.

Our first reaction was to ask what we could do to help Jennifer as she struggled. One answer was to listen to Jennifer, encouraging her to use her own voice to speak out and express her true self. Instead of striving to please others, she has been learning to focus on her own needs and desires. She has also been endeavoring to strengthen her own self-esteem. Her willingness to share with us and our willingness to listen as she works her way through this process provide important healing steps for all of us.

A second answer when searching for ways to help Jennifer came quickly from therapists: to help Jennifer, we ourselves had to be as healthy as possible in our own self images—in our relationship with each other—in our interactions with Jennifer.

One way of achieving that emotional health was to meet with Jennifer and her therapists, as requested by our daughter. During those sessions, Jennifer expressed childhood frustrations which surfaced as she searched for answers to the problems she was facing as an anorexic. Many of her childhood perceptions surprised us. Our love for Jennifer has always been deep, leading us as parents to take actions which we considered to be in her best interests. We have encouraged her to participate in activities she chose, to plan for her desired career, to find enjoyment in life. She, however, perceived these encouraging actions differently, feeling that she was caring for us. This was a jolting realization for us as parents: our intentions, designed to help our daughter, had actually crippled her when coupled with her intense need to caretake.

As a couple, we also entered counseling with a family therapist. Recommended as a counselor who works with family relationships of the eating disordered, our therapist enabled us to view Jennifer's illness and our involvement with patience and wisdom. Our relationships with one another and with Jennifer have been strengthened. We are more capable of recognizing troubling signs within relationships and of finding ways to approach those signals.

We recognize that Jennifer has moved beyond our home environment of father, mother, and two daughters. Over the years, she has surrounded herself with many others who are also impacting her life: her spouse, her extended family including in-laws, her friends, her coworkers, her church family. As discussed earlier, personal health is a key factor for anyone who is reaching out to the anorexic. All who are involved in Jennifer's life, if willing to strive for emotional and physical health, can improve their own lives as well as their relationships with Jennifer. Those healthy relationships demand a deep understanding of self and others, as well as a willingness to devote the serious efforts required for the building of those personal connections. Both understanding and effort are challenging, yet rewarding if achieved.

Ultimately, Jennifer's recovery is dependent upon her own clearly expressed voice. First, she must hear herself, and then she must strive to be heard by those around her. Recognizing this, we as parents watch her progress with great admiration. During the dark days of this illness, Jennifer continued to exhibit strength, choosing to take significant steps which have positively affected her recovery process. We see this book as another tangible look at the strength and determination which are part of Jennifer's true self. The poems and graphic art selections, as well as her carefully chosen words, provide insight into the struggles and the hopes of this young woman.

We love our daughter, Jennifer, and we pray that she finds health and happiness.

Richard and Julie Lane

My sister:

Jennifer is my only sibling and as sisters, we share a special bond. We have not always been emotionally close, particularly in our younger years, but as we've grown, I feel as if we've begun to understand and appreciate the special nature of a relationship that you share with someone who has, literally, known you for your entire life.

As a young girl, I remember looking up to Jen. She excelled at everything she attempted. She was a naturally talented athlete, musician, and student. I was taken in tow to countless sports games and tournaments over the course of the first 14 years of my life and became affectionately known as "Jen's little sister." All of the psychology books say that I should have resented her for being so talented; that I should have developed low self-esteem when I realized I couldn't live up to the exact standards my sister set. I should have hated being referred to as "Jennifer's little sister;" should have rebelled in some way against her "perfection." The truth is, I felt and did none of those things. I didn't mind being the little sister of such a talented girl. Turns out I wasn't a natural athlete but there were other things I was very good at. And as our interests began to diverge during our teenage years, I found it even easier to be proud of my sister.

We became particularly close in high school. My freshman year was Jen's senior year and I'm not sure what clicked at that moment in our lives, but suddenly, almost overnight it seemed, we became friends in addition to being sisters. That year of my life was special because of the closeness we shared and the time we spent together. To this day, when we are afforded the chance to spend rare time alone, that's the exact emotion I feel; the same feeling I had that whole year in high school. I've never experienced, nor do I expect to experience, that feeling with anyone else.

Living in the same household, growing up with the same set of parents and almost identical experiences in so many areas, I can't understand why Jen was struck with anorexia and not me. Not only can I not understand why Jen has to fight this and I don't, but I can't really understand what she's fighting at all. It's like I could always identify with her when she had the flu because I knew what that felt like and could help her get through it. But I can't identify with this. No matter how hard I try, sometimes I just want to tell her, "For God's sake, just eat. Why is that so hard?" I can't wrap my mind around how horrible this "thing" must be in order for her to knowingly deprive herself of food.

I've struggled to know what my role was in all of this. As a sibling, I could not nor should I have taken on the role of a parent or husband, but I was more than a friend. For the longest time, I couldn't figure out how I could help her. So many people were giving her advice about what to do; I didn't want to be just another voice in the crowd. And I was afraid to give advice because of my lack of ability to understand what it was she was fighting. I finally decided I needed to wait for her to come to me and let me know what she needed. Ultimately, that meant I pulled back from her for a time.

It was hard waiting for weeks and even months, feeling her slipping father from me, feeling our relationship become more distanced. But she did come to me a number of times and ask to talk things over from our childhood or journal with her about my experiences growing up. I've also had to come to the realization that this is Jen's war to win and no one else's. All the advice in the world doesn't matter. What matters is Jen coming to understand what she needs out of her relationships to be happy and fulfilled. No one can do that for her.

My message to her throughout this ordeal has been simple: She is strong enough to come out of this. I believe my sister is much stronger than many people make her out to be. And there's never been a single doubt in my mind that she would beat this. That's the honest truth. I think she needs space to work some things out for herself, but I don't think she needs to be treated as if she might break into a million pieces at any moment. I think she needs to stand up and be honest with herself and those in her life about what she needs. Relationships are negotiated and she has the power to determine how those relationships will fit into her life. That includes her relationship with me. She's always had this strength inside her; she just needs to rediscover it.

Karyn R. Stanley

My therapist:

What an honor and a privilege for me to be part of Jennifer's journey towards healing and "enoughness." Jennifer is an amazing woman who has walked her path with courage and determination. She has used incredible strength and resolve as well as creativity and humor to face one of the biggest challenges of her life. Thank you, Jennifer, for blessing me and so many others by sharing your personal journey in this book.

Eating disorder treatment is a long and rocky road. In many ways it is like embarking on a challenging hike, which is filled with both difficult and amazing experiences. The hike usually consists of incredibly difficult, painful stretches interspersed with plateaus filled with beauty and refreshment. It often seems that difficult issues are faced over and over again. However, the hope is that with ongoing work, these struggles will be faced each time with a new and different perspective because the hiker is at a higher elevation. Even after seeming to fall to a lower elevation, the hiker will have the experience and perspective of once having been at a higher level. Every time an issue is faced, the capacity to feel, make changes, and grow is strengthened.

Like Jennifer, so many women who struggle with disordered eating are bright, perceptive women who for a variety of reasons have learned to doubt these qualities in themselves. My experience with men with these issues is very limited, but I am sure that there are many similarities. If you are one of those people who struggle with disordered eating, please find ways to get help to be able to embrace yourself with love and respect. Help might include professional intervention through psychotherapy, nutritional therapy, medication, art therapy, and/or support groups but could also include such things as journaling, reading, and/or using creativity.

As a psychotherapist, I am just one part of an eating disorder treatment team that also includes a nutritionist as well as a physician and/or psychiatrist. Other members of the team might include a family therapist and art therapist. It is imperative that the team stay in close contact. As Jennifer described, there are many aspects of therapy such as providing support, helping to identify and learn to manage emotions, tracing and seeking healing from the roots of unhealthy beliefs and behaviors, establishing hope for the future including developing vision and goals, and developing and strengthening identity. The list of what might happen in psychotherapy could go on and on. As a therapist, I have the awesome privilege and responsibility of being a guide in this process.

Jennifer described in her book that her spiritual journey has been and continues to be an important part of her recovery. Jennifer and I share a common faith and have been able to do some amazing work around spiritual issues. She has relied on her faith while also being unafraid to question it and wrestle with difficult questions. This has resulted in a deepening of her spiritual life and an authenticity that adds to the richness of knowing her and spending time with her.

I believe that spirituality is a vital part of every person's recovery. Whatever the beliefs are, facing a crisis like an eating disorder causes questioning, and, hopefully, a difficulty staying noncommittal in the arena of faith. As Jennifer modeled, a willingness to struggle along with an openness to being available for God to work is invaluable. Seeking to make sense of life from a spiritual perspective sets the context in which much personal growth and healing can take place.

I do not know how to describe how blessed I am to be a part of Jennifer's journey. Thank you, Jen, for inviting me along. Always remember that you are enough just as you are.

Kim Lodewyk, Ph.D.
Clinical Psychologist

My nutritionist:

During my twenty years of working as a Nutrition Therapist with hundreds of people who struggle with eating issues and disordered eating, I have had the pleasure to work with few who are as dedicated to the process of recovery as Jen Calvin. Her story is remarkable in that it is her own. She continues to work diligently to discover ways to understand, challenge, and conquer the disorder that has come to reside within her. In the process she is finding her SELF in all her glory. Who knew she was an artist and a writer? Jen continues to learn how to use her voice, to accept and express her feelings, and to fuel her body.

In order for a person struggling with an eating disorder to benefit from nutrition therapy, she must challenge the notion that a number on a scale is indicative of who he or she is at the core. Ideas about how, what, and why a person eats a particular way are explored. Rigid myths about weight, food, and exercise are identified and replaced with the ability to intuitively choose what works for the individual. Jennifer has truly worked to make nutrition therapy work for her.

In this process we are all teachers and learners. Jen has taught me some very valuable lessons along this road including patience, persistence, and how to "live in the pause." It's been a pleasure to share this portion of her path with her. For this, and for her honest and inspiring story, I would like to thank her.

Kate Zager M.S. R.D. L.D.